Moving On

The Gypsies and Travellers of Britain

Moving On

The Gypsies and Travellers of Britain

DONALD KENRICK

AND

COLIN CLARK

University of Hertfordshire Press

Published in Great Britain by

University of Hertfordshire Press
Learning and Information Services
University of Hertfordshire
College Lane, Hatfield, Hertfordshire AL10 9AD.

ISBN 0 900458 99 2

Some of the material in this book was originally published in
On the Verge: the Gypsies of England by Donald Kenrick and
Sean Bakewell (Runnymede Trust, 1990;
University of Hertfordshire Press, 1995)

Design by Geoff Green Book Design, Cambridge CB4 5RA.

Cover photograph
Born in a bender tent but bringing up
her own family in a caravan on a council sit.
Myma Butler shown here holding her first grandchild is the little girl,
second on the left, in the picture of her parents and their family
taken outside their bender tent on Berkhampstead Common
on a snowy day in 1970.
Photograph by Bill Forster (see also Page 92)

Printed in Great Britain by J. W. Arrowsmith Ltd.

Moving On

Square pegs in round holes
yet ready for what life unfolds
we know what the future holds
for the Gypsies
it is the gift for precious few
but the Gypsies know,
Move on, that's what the Gypsies will do.

Laughter will shatter the ruins of the world
you'll hear it from the Gypsies
and music will prevail,
when the caged birds are silenced,
music from the Gypsies.
 Mothers singing beyond walls and over waters
the voice of the Gypsies.
And the young will renew the old
as memories are retold, retold
for what is time to all of we
for we are every Romany.

Move on again, Yes that's what we do,
and we will find a tale or two.
The old world is our breath, our heart

and our start, is where we finish
forever, moving on.

Hester Hedges
*Hester Hedges is a Gypsy girl
studying law at De Montfort University*

Contents

Appendices

Tables and graphs

Illustrations

Introduction

Gypsies and Travellers in Britain are at a crisis point where the survival of their way of life into the new millennium is in doubt. For many families life is no easier than that described in the pamphlet written thirty years ago by Grattan Puxon for the National Council for Civil Liberties, *On the Road,* or in the two editions of *On the Verge* which this volume replaces.

In these pages we give a description of the Gypsy and Traveller population of Britain as it is, as well as of the stereotypes that abound and show how, although harassed as a minority, they have not, in practice, had the protection which the law should afford to minorities. Gypsies and other Travellers are still 'on the verge' of society. We discuss the legislation that has been brought in to control their movements and review their relationships with the police as well as local and central government agencies. Finally, we look at the emerging interest the European organisations are taking in the nomad populations.

We have chosen a new title as this is, in many ways, a new book with new co-authors. Some of the material from the earlier editions of the pamphlet *On the Verge* have been retained as has the intention of producing a readable text for the general public as well as those involved with Gypsies and Travellers in their work. There are completely new chapters on New Travellers, Private Sites, Scotland, and Wales. Many of the examples of harassment, prejudice and media treatment are also new and, happily, in bringing other sections up to date, we have come across new government initiatives and court decisions which give us some grounds for optimism. We hope that Gypsies and Travellers will continue to move on, but only of their own free will.

New Labour had been a disapointment to Gypsies even before Home Secretary Jack Straw's vacuous remarks about "real Romanies" being superior to people "who masquerade as Travellers or Gypsies". His Department's much vaunted Good Practice Guidlines for evictions have been ignored by police and local authorities throughout the country. We hope that Gypsies and Travellers will continue to move on, but only of their own free will.

Donald Kenrick and Colin Clark

Acknowledgements

This study incorporates some of the material that appeared in the two editions of *On the Verge*. The chapter on Wales has been contributed by Rachel Morris and we thank her for taking the time to write this. Colin Clark, the main author of the chapter on Scotland, wishes to thank Michelle Lloyd in Edinburgh for her helpful input and critical comments on an earlier version of that chapter. Colin was also the main author of the chapter on New Travellers and he thanks Alan Dearling for his helpful comments. Thanks also to 'The Levellers' for permission to reproduce the lyrics for their song 'Battle of the Beanfield'.

We would like to acknowledge the help we have had in revising the text from Clare Paul and to thank Sian Bakewell, much of whose contribution to the first edition has been retained.

Thanks are also due to Thomas Acton, Penny Bollinger, Sandra Clay, Alan Dearling, Arthur Ivatts, Betty Jordan, Judith Okely, Jim Spiller, Diana Allen and Gillian Taylor for helpful comments on various draft versions of all or parts of the text. We also extend our gratitude to a number of local health visitors, to the many photographers who made their pictures available without any charge and to all members of the e-mail discussion lists Romnet and Traveller-Acad for their contributions and all we have learned from them. Please keep those e-mails coming.

The new parts of the book written by Colin Clark are dedicated by him, with love, to Margaret and Fergus.

It goes almost without saying that both authors would also like to acknowledge the help, patience and motivation of Bill Forster of the University of Hertfordshire Press in producing this book.

Donald Kenrick and Colin Clark

The authors

Donald Kenrick has worked in adult education and as an adviser to Gypsy civil rights organisations. He is co-author of *Gypsies under the Swastika* (1995), an overall study of the Nazi persecution of Gypsies, and has written widely on the Romani language. His historical study *Gypsies from India to the Mediterranean* (1993) has been translated into eight languages. He is Vice-President of the Gypsy Council for Education, Culture, Welfare and Civil Rights

Colin Clark works as a lecturer in social policy at the University of Newcastle upon Tyne. As well as teaching Romani studies, he has conducted research and writes about the contemporary situation of Gypsies and other Travellers in the UK and Europe. He has a particular interest in New Travellers and the Romanies in Central and Eastern Europe and has published chapters and articles in a variety of academic books and journals. He is a member of the Gypsy Council for Education, Culture, Welfare and Civil Rights and other Gypsy civil rights organisations.

Foreword

After a lifetime involved with Gypsy issues it is my opinion that our way of life has never been in so much danger as it is today from institutionalised racism and xenophobia. New legislation is making it more difficult for Gypsy and Travelling people to live in their traditional areas. The Criminal Justice and Public Order Act (1994) has forced families either to leave the road or to keep 'moving on', which inevitably brings them into conflict with the law.

It is reassuring to read this impressive new book, *Moving On*, which replaces *On the Verge*. It begins with a poem by a young Romany girl which shows how our younger people feel today and goes on to cover all the most important aspects of life as a Gypsy today from our early history to the struggle for sites, health, education and civil rights.

It will be a valuable resource for colleges and universities with courses on the study of ethnic minorities and for the public who want to discover the reality of life as a Gypsy today, the true story behind the often racist headlines in local papers.

Peter Mercer MBE
General Secretary, East Anglian Gypsy Council
Hon. Vice-President, Gypsy Council
for Education, Culture, Welfare and Civil Rights
Member of the Presidium of the International Romany Union.

Foreword to *On the Verge: the Gypsies of England* (1990, 1995)

When I first read this book it made a welcome change from the usual reports full of statistics for academics and romantic stories about camp-fires and hedgehogs. As well as some history and law, there are first-hand stories showing what the travelling life is really like – as told by Gypsies themselves.

The situation of our people in Britain has got worse with new laws, and our traditional way of life is under attack. So, I welcome this new edition which is full of valuable information for those who want to understand our problems.

Peter Mercer
Secretary, East Anglian Gypsy Council
Representative of Britain on the Presidium of the International Romany Union

Glossary

Flattie A term used by Scottish Travellers and Showpeople for a house-dweller.

Gorgio A Romany term meaning someone who is not a Romany.

Gypsy An abbreviation of the word 'Egyptian', a name given to the Romany people in the Middle Ages as it was thought they came from Egypt. The word is not in itself derogatory and we use it throughout as the general term for anyone of nomadic habit of life.

Romany As a noun: a member of a nomadic people originating in North India, the Romanies. Also an adjective relating to the culture, customs and language of the Romanies. It is derived from the word 'Rom' (plural 'Roma')

Romani The language of the Romanies

Traveller
1. An Irish or Scottish nomad
2. An overall term for nomads covering Romany Gypsies as well as Irish, New and Scottish Travellers

In all quotations the forms 'gipsy' or 'gypsy' have been standardised to 'Gypsy', and 'Traveller' capitalised.

Caravan The term caravan (as defined by the 1960 Caravan Sites Act) includes a mobile home comprising a maximum of two units which is – in spite of the name – not mobile. It is brought on to a site in two parts on a lorry and put together on site. It cannot be towed by a lorry and for practical purposes (as opposed to legal niceties) is the same as a chalet.

Mobile home site A site consisting entirely of mobile homes, popular with retired people or for holidays. Gypsies are rarely allowed on these sites.

1

A profile of the Gypsy and Traveller community

Who are the Gypsies?

The present day Gypsy population of the Britain can be divided into five main groups, each with its own cultural heritage and identity.

The Romanies or 'Romany chals' of England and South Wales

The largest group numbering about 63,000 – including house-dwelling families. They previously spoke a dialect of Romani but now speak a variety of English using many Romani words. They are descendants of Romanies (known as 'Egyptians') who came to England from the Continent in the Sixteenth and Seventeenth centuries. Some intermarriage with Gorgios (non-Romanies) has taken place, but earlier customs are still preserved. In particular, different sorts of washing are kept separate, and often the possessions of the dead are burnt or otherwise destroyed.

The Kalé of North Wales

Some 1,000 persons, descendants of the Woods and other families who migrated from the south-west of England to Wales in the Seventeenth and Eighteenth centuries. Up to a few years ago they continued to speak inflected Romani (with endings changing for tense and case). Most are now living in houses in Wales.

The Roma: Romanies who have come to England this century

They include Coppersmiths whose grandparents came here in the 1930s and Hungarian Romanies, most of whom arrived as refugees after 1956. The majority of the some 2,000 Roma now live in houses but the women still wear the traditional long dresses and ornaments. The Coppersmiths, at least, keep up Romani as their main language, often telling neighbours they are Greeks, to avoid discrimination.

The term 'Gypsy' in the 1960 Caravan Sites Act includes two other nomadic groups, and New Travellers (see Chapter 6) who follow a similar lifestyle.

Irish Travellers. A nomadic group from Ireland

Some say they are the descendants of peasants driven off their lands by Cromwell but there is historical and linguistic evidence for placing their origin as a separate ethnic group much earlier, even before the coming of the Celts to Ireland. They now speak a variety of English.

It is estimated that 19,000 live in Britain, including many born over here. The majority travel in caravans. Although Irish immigration to England began several centuries ago the first reliable report of the presence of Irish Travellers dates from 1850. After the Second World War many men came over to work on the motorways and later as labourers for local councils, as well as scrap metal dealers. Travelling women could pass as ordinary Irish and get work in hospitals, which was not so easy in Ireland itself because of prejudice.

On the whole the Irish Travellers have found it more difficult than the Romany chals to get pitches on local authority caravan sites. In February 1993, a conservative MP called for the mass deportation of Irish Travellers to the Republic.

Scottish Travellers.

A nomadic group formed in Scotland in the period 1500-1800 from intermarriage and social integration between local nomadic craftsmen and immigrant Romanies from France and Spain in particular. At any given time there may be several hundred Scottish Travellers visiting England, while Liverpool has a small house-dwelling population of Scottish Travellers. It is estimated that some 20,000 Scottish Travellers live in Scotland, both on sites and in houses. Families living on both sides of the border with England form a distinct group within the Scottish Traveller community.

In Table A below, we have calculated the population figures for Gypsies in Britain. We arrive at a total figure of 120,000 people. These figures have been derived from a mixture of official statistics (e.g., census counts) and various other sources (e.g., non-governmental organisations).

Table A: Population figures
Estimated overall numbers of each group in Britain

Romanies (Romany chals)	63,000
Kalé	1,000
Roma	2,000
Irish Travellers	19,000
Scottish Travellers	20,000
New Travellers	15,000
TOTAL	120,000

In Table B on the next page we show the *official figures* for Gypsy caravans in England. We consider a more accurate figure for unauthorised caravans in England to be over 4,000.

The counts are conducted in January and July each year. The January figures give a better picture of the caravan-dwelling population as the July figures include house-dwelling Gypsies who travel in the summer only and caravans which have a council or private pitch but which are recorded as being on an unauthorised encampment during the summer. The figures for July 1998 are: 3,700 unauthorised; 5,997 council; 3,848 private; 13,545 total.

Possibly as many as 10 per cent of the caravans on unauthorised sites are on land owned by Gypsies but without planning permission. In most cases they will be under the threat of enforcement action for their owners to remove them.

Table B: Official figures for caravans in England		
	Jan 1989	Jan 1999
Unauthorised	3,740	2,568
Council sites	5,159	6,162
Private sites	2,422	4,279
Total	11,321	13,009

In the table below we give the *official* figures for Gypsy caravans in Wales. Since 1997 there has not been a count.

Table C: Official figures for caravans in Wales		
	Jan 1990	Jan 1997
Unauthorised	182	217
Council sites	471	502
Private sites	39	13
Total	692	732

The table opposite shows the figures for caravans in Scotland. The 1992 figure comes from the official count conducted by the Scottish Office Central Research Unit *Counting Travellers in Scotland: the 1992 picture.* The July 1998 figures are based on information contained within the recent document *Travelling People in Scotland: Report on Seasonal Count July 1998* which was again produced by the Scottish Office Central Research Unit in November 1998.

Travellers in Northern Ireland

There are, according to government figures, approximately 112 Irish Traveller families in Northern Ireland and this gives a figure of some 2,000 people. They live on serviced sites, roadside encampments and in houses. This figure of 2,000 includes those house-dwelling families. Apart from two families of Romany origin and visiting Scottish Travellers, all the nomads are Irish Travellers. The largest single concen-

Table D: Figures for caravans / Traveller households in Scotland (1)		
	Mar/Apr 1992	July 1998
Unauthorised	165	137
Council sites	270	285
Private sites	105	158
Total	540 (2)	580

Notes

1. The above figures for Scotland, produced by the Scottish Office Central Research Unit, often confuse the number of caravans with the number of families, individuals and pitches. Clear figures are not easy to uncover in these reports and the figures, on face value, can be misleading. Like most statistical data, they should be treated with caution and some scepticism. Many organisations that work with Travellers in Scotland consider the above figures to be very low.

2. It should be noted that the 1969 estimate of a total Traveller population of 450 households throughout Scotland was derived from counts at two seasons and a number of scaling factors. Applying similar scaling methods to the March 1992 count gives an estimated total of between 750 and 800 Traveller households in Scotland at that time.

tration is based around West Belfast although there are groupings in places like Craigavon, Newry and Omagh.

The circuit followed by nomadic families is small and the majority spend all the year in the North, although most, if not all, have relatives in the Republic. Having said this, there is some seasonal movement by some families over to England and Scotland, as well as to the Republic.

The 1968 Caravan Sites Act did not apply to Northern Ireland, but there has been some progress towards building caravan sites and there are now four.

The recent Race Relations (Northern Ireland) Order 1997 has made it illegal to discriminate against anyone on the grounds of race. This legislation covers all minority ethnic and racial groups, including Irish Travellers. The Order, like the 1976 Race Relations Act, covers discrimination in a variety of settings and contexts. For example, discrimination in employment, education, housing, the provision of goods, services and facilities. The Commission for Racial Equality for Northern Ireland has the job of dealing with problems that arise in these areas.

A brief history of the Romanies

North-west India formed the cradle of the Romany nation. This much at least is accepted by the majority of those who have attempted to reconstruct the history of this people. Possibly they existed as a loose confederation of nomadic craftsmen and entertainers following a pattern similar to groups such as the Banjara and Sapera (Kalbelia) in modern India. Possibly such a confederation formed during their stay in the Middle East. No contemporary accounts exist of the first Romanies to reach Persia but the poet Firdausi and other authors in the tenth century write of the arrival of Indian entertainers five hundred years earlier. Linguistic and other evidence suggests that the Romanies of Europe belong to groups that left India over a thousand years ago. They spent a comparatively short time in the Middle East. At no time did they move in a solid mass from east to west but their pattern of migration was probably similar to that of today with family groups moving at different speeds, according to local circumstances and opportunity for work.

The first families recorded in Eastern Europe arrived from Asia Minor and earned their living as bootmakers and metalworkers. Eastern Europe has continued to have a large settled Romany population, usually called 'Tsigani', in contrast to Western Europe where the word 'Gypsy' is synonymous with 'nomad.' The first authenticated records of their presence in Britain are in 1505 for Scotland and 1514 for Lambeth in England. However, since two ladies apparently dressed up as Romanies for a court masked ball in England as early as 1510 it is possible that real Romanies had been in the country for some years before then.

The common people welcomed these newcomers who performed many useful services in town and country and provided entertainment as a welcome relief from the routine of everyday life. However, the Romanies soon aroused the hostility of powerful enemies. The Church resented the competition of palm readers, the Guilds the fact that the nomads could undercut their prices and the State wanted them to settle down, register their names and birthdates and occupy a fixed position in the system. Soon after their arrival, the English Parliament passed an Act under which all 'Egipcions' in the country were to leave within sixteen days and further immigration was prohibited. Later legislation introduced the death penalty for the sole crime of 'being a Gypsy'. The extent to which these laws were applied varied from one part of the country to another but men and women were executed in Aylesbury, Durham and York.

After 1780, anti-Gypsy legislation was gradually repealed. Tolerated when they were useful as farm labourers, blacksmiths or entertainers and made to move on when their services were no longer needed, the Gypsies survived on the margins of society until the outbreak of World War II in 1939.

With the outbreak of war and subsequent conscription of able-bodied men and women the Gypsies became a useful source of labour for the war effort. Men were called up to the army and women recruited for land work and the munitions factories. Unable to read and travelling from place to place, many young men never received their 'call-up papers'. Police rounded them up. Once in uniform, Romanies, as in the First World War, fought heroically, winning many medals, such as Jack Cunningham V.C. They were particularly valued as snipers and scouts, both in Europe and the Far East.

The war had a dark side too. A soldier might come home on leave to

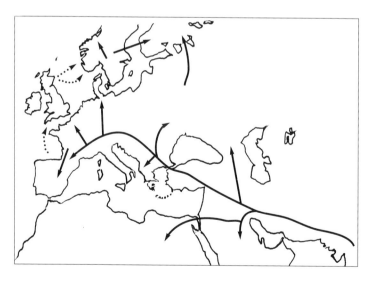

Map showing migration route of Roma from India.

find his caravan site had been broken up by the police and he had to return to barracks not knowing where his family was, whether they were still alive or perhaps had been killed in a bombing raid.

It is often forgotten that, in addition to the Jews, Nazi Germany tried to wipe out Romanies, homosexuals, socialists, trades unionists, Jehovah's Witnesses and persons with disabilities. Some Romanies were aware that, across the Channel, Hitler's Germany was planning to annihilate them. In 1942, preparatory to a planned invasion of Britain, the Central Security Office in Berlin started to collect information on the Romany population of England.

The war over, there was a brief period after 1945 when Gypsies were able to live at peace with their house-dwelling neighbours. The coming to power of a Labour Government brought a new tolerance generally towards minorities; casual work was available for all with post-war reconstruction and, with many bombed-out or demobilised families living in prefabricated houses or mobile homes, the Gypsies in their caravans were no longer an anomaly. However, within a few years a shortage of land arose and led to problems as we shall see below.

Work

Success in most European countries is viewed in terms of career achievements. In Romany society as a whole, however, work is considered not to be an end in itself but a means of earning money while staying economically independent. Independence requires mobility and adaptability. Gypsies have the power to adjust and have adapted their trades successfully to growing industrialisation. They rarely have one single occupation but practice a combination of trades, such as scrap collecting, tarmac'ing, hawking, fortune-telling and so on. These trades also require a minimum of tools, which in turn enables them to stay mobile.

In contrast with sedentary people, Gypsies of all the groups have until recently not sought permanent jobs as this would go against their preference for the flexibility of self-employment. They generally work as a domestic or family unit and will, therefore, rarely have the need to employ others. This way of working also enables them to avoid becoming employees which would entail having a fixed address. Sedentarisation can occur at either end of the economic scale. When

The two biggest events in the year are the fairs at Stowe (May) and Appleby (June) where Gypsies meet members of their extended families, do business and young people have an opportunity to form relationships.

Two horse traders discuss the days business alongside the trotting track at Appleby; *photograph by David Gallant*

Two Irish Traveller girls amused by the camera at Stowe Fair; *photograph by David Gallant*

prosperous, a Gypsy may open a business such as a scrap yard or plant nursery that in turn demands the employment of labour and a fixed abode. Also, when destitute or tied to a site with no work area a Gypsy may have to resort to accepting a permanent job.

Seasonal work provides an ideal source of income. Particularly in rural areas where fruit and vegetable pickers are still needed, Gypsy families constitute an ideal labour force. They appear when work needs doing and disappear when it is finished. They provide their own accommodation and are not likely to go on strike for higher wages.

Patterns of movement and work vary, which cutdown on competition from other Gypsies but it is dangerous to generalise. However, traditionally, Gypsies winter in one place and may then set off shortly after Easter for early farm work, such as picking daffodils in the West Country and touring around to see when soft fruit is likely to be ready. June brings Epsom Races for fortune-telling and horse-dealing or just meeting friends and relatives. Some may go instead to the big horse-fair at Appleby or stop in Cambridge during the *Midsummer Fair*.

Many of the traditional fairs that Gypsies visit, such as Doncaster St Leger, have been closed down. All without exception are under threat from local councils who dislike the influx of caravan dwellers to their areas. Barnet, Horsmonden, Newcastle Hoppings, Stow on the Wold and others survive from year to year, although in a much reduced form. These gatherings serve several functions for the Romany community who trade among themselves, particularly for horses and harnesses, which will then be sold elsewhere at a profit. They also provide an opportunity for young people to meet and are vital if the community is to survive. New Travellers have found a similar problem with their festivals (see chapter six for further details).

In mid-summer, work is to be found at the seaside, telling fortunes for the women, moving deck chairs by lorry for the men. Otherwise, a dry summer is ideal for repairing roofs, landscape gardening and gate-making. Autumn brings a chance for plum and potato picking and then it is back to the edge of a town to seek a suitable site for the winter.

Work patterns distinguish the Romanies and Travellers from other groups of migrant workers who rarely remain as independent of wage labour as the Gypsies. Unfortunately, nomadism combined with the avoidance of conventional employment and their dependence on the sedentary population, has conjured up the unfounded stereotype of the Gypsies as parasites. There has to be symbiosis – demand from the house-dwelling population for the goods and services the nomads supply – and both sides benefit from these transactions.

In caravans and houses

Nomadism is the most notable feature of the Romany lifestyle in Britain and one that has perhaps created the most misunderstanding. The image of the 'wandering Gypsies', alien everywhere they roam, has hounded them in the past in every country through which they have travelled. This nomadism is in contrast with modern European society where the populace remains largely sedentary.

Not all Romany Gypsies are nomads and not all nomads are Romany Gypsies and a Gypsy is not merely 'a member of a wandering race' as defined by the Oxford English Dictionary. Some Gypsies live their lives by the seasons, as previously mentioned. They may remain sedentary in the winter months and then travel in the spring, while others may stay in the same place for several years, moving only ten or fifteen times in their lives. Yet a third pattern is for families to move all the time if they have occupations which require a continual supply of new customers. Some travel throughout the British Isles while others will never leave a particular county. Nomadism is a state of mind rather than a state of action. Even when sedentary a Romany remains a nomad in his values and spirit. If he buys a bungalow he may well keep a small touring caravan in the backyard, just in case.

During a survey conducted by Cardiff Law School, an Area Housing Manager in Wales commented:

> There have been numerous traveller families waiting for Local Authority housing for years but after they had been living in the house for a short while they found they were unable to settle to the different lifestyle. There have been cases where the family had moved into a house but in fact had chosen to live in the caravan parked in the garden.

A resident on the Cardiff Gypsy site said:

> It would be wrong to put Gypsies into houses, They would be taking away all our culture. And we wouldn't be able to keep pets: chickens and

horses. I'd feel lost in a house 'cause of all the space, it would make me feel ill.

A Romany settled in a house may still be referred to as a Traveller by other Romanies, for, in addition to its practical functions, nomadism is a part of Romany identity and distinguishes them from the Gorgios. It has helped Gypsies in Britain to safeguard their culture as it has enabled them to avoid too much contact with the non-Romany. They travel not because they are asocial or anti-social but because travel is part of their heritage. In the debate leading up to the 1968 Caravan Sites Act, Parliament accepted this and proposed the setting up of a national network of sites between which Gypsies could move and preserve their way of life. Many Gypsies moved on to these sites as they opened, thinking they would be able to move from place to place, but now, increasingly, stay put because there is nowhere for them to move to, as there are insufficient pitches. Table B above shows that upwards of 2,500 Gypsy families have nowhere to stop. This lack of spaces on authorised caravan sites and the consequent harassment they encounter on roadside encampments is a major problem for Gypsies in Britain today.

Local authorities have at times attempted settlement policies to alleviate what they see as the 'Gypsy problem'. A few have been well-intentioned and have aimed at improving the poor living conditions that some Gypsies had to endure. One such example was the setting up of centres in the 1960s by Hampshire County Council. Many Gypsies who had been living in huts took advantage of these centres that provided them initially with basic accommodation. If they showed a willingness to assimilate to house-dwelling society by abandoning their dogs and their distinctive colourful clothing, normal council housing accommodation was offered.

In other cases, local authorities have been reluctant to accommodate those Gypsies who wish to be housed although the Homeless Persons Act gives them this duty in the case of any Gypsy without a legal pitch. A south London council demanded that one family (who had registered as homeless) stay on their illegal site until the bailiffs (acting under the order of the same council) arrived, then leave their caravan and report to the Housing Office. However, even if families are technically ruled to be 'intentionally homeless', they can now, if there are children, be housed under certain sections of the Children Act.

This reluctance to house Gypsies is, in some cases, due to fear of hostility by the local population towards their future Gypsy neighbours. A poll in 1963 conducted by Gallup found that 60 per cent of Britons do not want to live next to Gypsies, a higher percentage than for any other ethnic minority. This hostility sometimes comes out into the open.

Margaret M. and her five children wanted to move from the official caravan site in Winterbourne into a council house in Bristol for the sake of her son who suffered from kidney problems and had undergone a brain operation. The potential neighbours organised a protest meeting in a local school, attended by more than 100 people. Following this, the housing department decided to review the offer.

Mrs B describes her experiences:

> I was put into temporary accommodation in a very high class area and the neighbours didn't like us because we are Gypsies, even though we have not said any wrong or bad words against anyone. The neighbours started to complain about rubbish but the rubbish wasn't ours. It was there before we moved in. And also our dog, but he is a puppy and couldn't make a loud bark if he tried. They also said we have been threatening them but we haven't. The neighbours twice complained to the police that we had stolen electrical goods in the house and the police broke down the door while we were out. But they found nothing. Now we are told we have to leave because of our 'anti-social behaviour' and the council will not re-house us.

Of greater importance than possible hostility from neighbours in the comparatively low take-up of housing are the psychological problems that the Gypsies themselves may face at the prospect of permanent housing. Housing takes away any possibility of freedom and mobility which Gypsies want. Working from a house has its problems, too. A Gypsy in Essex was refused permission to conduct a car valeting service in his extensive grounds, although the nearest neighbour was a lorry park on the opposite side of the road.

One Romany family said that they concealed their origins and were accepted by their neighbours. Then, suspicions were aroused by the vans the Gypsies parked outside their house, visits by relatives with dark faces and the women's long dresses. Their identity revealed, they were ostracised by the neighbours and in the end moved back into caravans.

Not all experience hostility and, if entered into for positive reasons, such as stable education for the children or a more secure environment for their elderly parents, housing can be successful. It seems, however, that a large proportion of those Gypsies who go into housing do so for negative reasons, to escape harassment or as a result of poverty. As Elizabeth Davies pointed out in one of the very few studies of this topic, the help of local authority workers to make the transition into housing a smooth one is often not available and the result is that many Gypsies leave housing within a short period of time and return to the road.

Table E: Moving into housing
Number of families who moved into housing

	From authorised sites	From unauthorised sites	Total
1981-4	248	275	523
1985	84	112	196

Number of families moving back into caravans
(1981-5):   146

From E. Davies, *Gypsies and Housing.* Department of Environment, 1987

Travellers without 'trailers'

There are large communities of Romany descent living in houses. Some of these families were placed in council housing in the 1930s, others from the 1960s onwards, as the caravan sites where they lived were closed down by the local authorities. Some may still keep a 'trailer' – a touring caravan – in the back garden. Many will have a stone horse or a large wheel on the front wall.

Bromley, in Kent, houses many families who were displaced when sites on Belvedere Marshes and elsewhere were closed after 1945. Part of Mitcham was known as Redskin Village because of the large numbers of Romanies who wintered in yards there while travelling to Kent for fieldwork in the summer. Many of these settled in flats when the yards closed – although some of these took advantage of the first sites to be built in south London after the 1968 Caravan Sites Act and moved back into caravans. Another town with a cohesive settled Romany population is Southampton.

Such family trees as have been published and the authors' personal knowledge of families suggests that about half of each generation of Romanies has moved into housing, certainly during the twentieth century.

The proportion of Irish Travellers in housing may be higher. In Manchester there are over 350 housed Irish Traveller children registered with the education service, compared to some 150 from the official and roadside sites. As the definition of Traveller for education purposes omits those who have been living in houses for over two years, the actual number is probably higher. A number of Travellers from County Mayo used to come to Lincoln after 1945 to harvest potatoes and sugar beet and many of these settled in the town.

No comprehensive research exists on this subject, but we tried to estimate and include the house-dwelling 'Traveller' population in Table E opposite.

Immigrants and refugees

In the last two years, Labour Home Secretary Jack Straw has tried to stop Slovak Romanies from the Czech Republic coming to Britain. About 200 Romanian Romanies have also attempted to come to Britain in recent months. It was some years ago that governments of both parties began to try and control immigration, including that of Gypsies. In July 1966, for example, fifteen families coming from the Continent with caravans were stopped at Southampton and sent back to Europe. Two other large groups were refused entry in 1970 and 1975. Since the setting-up of the European Community, Gypsies from Western Europe have the right to come here. However, this does not mean the right to a place on a caravan site or to ply their traditional trades as they cannot obtain peddlers' licences without which they may not sell in the street or from house to house.

Many Romanies were amongst the people in continental Europe who found themselves stateless after World War II. Although the United Kingdom signed the Convention on Stateless Persons (1954) which reads 'The contracting countries shall as far as possible facilitate the assimilation and naturalisation of stateless persons,' in practice the Home Office ignores this Convention. To take one current case of many:

Mrs D. is a stateless Romany whose husband has a French passport. He can come here freely as a European Community citizen but she has been allowed to enter only for six months each calendar year.

The Home Office has stated:

> The existence of the Committee of Experts on Stateless Nomads on which the United Kingdom is represented and the Council of Europe's resolutions on stateless nomads do not preclude stateless nomads from the requirement to qualify to enter or remain in the United Kingdom under the Immigration Rules. The recommendations of the Council of Europe about nomads do not, in our view, put them in a special position in relation to the exercise of immigration control. We will continue to treat nomad applicants no more or less favourably than anyone else.

In recent years Romanies from Eastern Europe have tried to get asylum because of racial attacks in their own countries. The attitude of the Home Office is that there may be 'harassment' of Romanies but this does not amount to 'persecution' and so the applicants are refused and sent back to where they came from. Letters of refusal follow a regular model as in this correspondence with a Slovak Romany:

> The Secretary of State takes the view that skinheads cannot be regarded as 'agents of persecution' within the terms of the [1951 United Nations] Convention [relating to the Status of Refugees]. He considers that the incidents which you have described are localised and random in nature. In order to bring yourself within the scope of the Convention you would have to show that these incidents were not simply the random actions of individuals but were a sustained pattern or campaign of persecution directed at you which was controlled, sanctioned or condoned by the authorities or that the authorities were unable or unwilling to offer you protection.

This, despite recent murders in Banska Bystrica and Handlova in Slovakia and in the Czech Republic between 1990 and 1996 when over twenty Romanies were killed in racist attacks. Every month twenty serious attacks are reported. In the event, some adjudicators have reversed the decisions of the immigration officer, on the grounds that the governments of the Czech and Slovak governments in particular are unable to protect Romany citizens from the attacks by skinheads. Additionally, a small number of Romanies holding Yugoslav papers and unable to return to Bosnia because of the fighting have been allowed to stay.

A new 130 clause Immigration and Asylum Bill was published by the Labour Home Secretary Jack Straw in February 1999. It is the most comprehensive and radical overhaul of the entry system to Britain in thirty years. According to Straw, the package of measures will cut down on the slow and cumbersome system of determining asylum applications. Currently there is a backlog of some 76,000 applications in the UK. Those at the bottom of the pile face a wait of years for a decision.

The most radical measure is the ending of the rights that asylum seekers have to social security benefits whilst they wait for their decision. Instead, they are to be given accommodation and support in the form of vouchers for food. Asylum seekers are to be given little say in where they live; most will be forced to go where they are told to by Home Office ministers. Historically, asylum seekers and refugees have settled in the south-east and London. The new measures effectively end this and distribute new arrivals throughout the country.

One of the other main measures is concerned with what was called the 'White List'. This is a list of a number of countries from where any asylum-seekers coming to the UK are presumed to be and treated as 'bogus'. This list includes countries such as Romania and Pakistan.

There are also some clauses that deal with the running and work of detention centres, principally to do with increasing the powers of the wardens. A new 'one-stop' appeal process is to be introduced, simplifying a process involving many stages.

As well as registrars, immigration officers are given even tougher powers of detection, search, fingerprinting and arrest. Lorry drivers can be fined up to £2,000 per immigrant for bringing in clandestine entrants. This clause was introduced to the Bill after some 106 Romanies from Romania were found to have gained illegal entry to Britain in the backs of lorries in December 1998.

It seems very likely that this Bill will become an Act in the near future.

Travelling Showpeople

It has been said that Travelling Showpeople are Britain's 'last lost tribe'. They total some 21,000 – 25,000 people and, like Romanies, have their own language and culture. They also tend to marry within the extended group.

Showpeople are commercial nomads who move from town to town during the fair season which lasts from February through to November. During the height of the season it is not uncommon for some 250 fairs to be held each week in the larger towns.

Ancient charters dating from the Middle Ages give Showpeople the right to pitch their rides, shows and stalls in certain places at certain times. These often coincide with saints days and feasts. For example, Stratford was granted a charter in 1196 and a statute protects this fair. It would take an Act of Parliament to stop the fair taking place on Stratford's streets.

The fairs act as a fixed point in what is, by definition, a highly nomadic life. For Showpeople families, such as the Kemps, the Robinsons, the Noyces and the Clarks, they are a social as well as economic calendar. Life events, such as births, marriages and deaths, can all be related to dates of fairs in various parts of the country.

As with Gypsies, the Showpeople's way of life has long been seen as being out of date and redundant. The end of the fairs has been regularly predicted almost since they first started. In the mid nineteenth century the historian Thomas Frost argued that the fairs were becoming extinct due to the new attractions that the 'Flatties' (settled people) were being entertained by: the music halls, zoological gardens and aquariums. He suggested that 'the last Showmen will soon be as great a curiosity as the dodo'. It is clear, however, that the Showpeople in the Twentieth century have survived and continued to prosper 'despite the telly' as one showman put it.

Some of the legislation affecting Gypsies in Britain has also affected Showpeople and viceversa. It was the Showpeople's resistance to the 1889 Movable Dwellings Bill that led to the creation of the Van Dwellers Association (VDA). The VDA was later to become known as the Showmen's Guild that today both represents and governs the Showpeople. It has a membership of some 5,000 and almost all of these are men. Nearly all the fairs in Britain are run under the auspices of the Guild. More recent legislation, like the Caravan Sites Act of 1968, never applied to Showpeople (or circus people). In theory, their situation in relation to the 1994 Criminal Justice and Public Order Act is just as precarious as it is for Gypsies and New Travellers.

Tradition and heritage are two common words used to justify, support and legitimise both the fairs and Showpeople themselves. With local authorities and district councils constantly closing down such events, the Showpeople require a solid defence to protect their livelihood and very way of life.

2

Wales

Introduction

The laws and regulations which apply to Gypsies and Travellers in England with respect to accommodation, eviction, planning, education and health apply equally to those in Wales; although Welsh Office Circulars have different numbers from their equivalents in England, their content is identical.

In their book *The Welsh Gypsies: Children of Abram Wood* Professor and Mrs Jarman assert that there are probably no true Romany Gypsies now travelling in Wales. They go on to say that the few Romany families travelling the roads in Britain have fallen on hard times owing to the lack of camping sites. It is possible that some Welsh farmers would still be prepared to allow small numbers of Gypsies known to them to camp on their land had the recent influx of Irish Travellers with their different ways not brought about a hardening of attitudes towards all nomads. The way of life of these recently arrived nomads – not to mention the New Travellers – who refuse to conform with the more stereotyped and urbanised society of the twentieth century, arouses much resentfulness and intolerance.

The view 'it's not the real Gypsies that bother me, it's the other ones' appears to be prevalent among the settled population throughout the UK. Angus Fraser goes as far as to say in the Introduction to his work *The Gypsies:*

> If a people is a group of men, women and children with a common language, a common culture and a common racial type, who can be readily

distinguished from their neighbours, it is a long time since the Gypsies
were that. They have, over the centuries, become remarkably diversified.
So too have the meanings attached to the term 'Gypsy' itself – a semantic
problem not of the Gypsies' making. The word is the name (or rather, one
of many names) given to them by outsiders.

This term is, of course, used by the Gypsies themselves in Britain. At
least in South Wales it is probably true that most of the Travellers are
Irish. The south coast of Wales is a corridor through which Irish
Travellers pass on their way from the Republic of Ireland to the Welsh
ports and on to work and family in England; some stay and settle here. It
is difficult to know how many Travelling people in Wales are 'Gypsies'
in the Romany sense; for the purposes of social justice, it may not even
matter. What is significant are the problems of impaired access to appropriate accommodation, health and education services, and the lack of
respect for difference on the part of settled people, experienced by all
Travelling people (including those now in houses).

Numbers

The January 1996 Gypsy Count Survey in Wales, undertaken by local
authorities and collated by the Welsh Office, estimated that there had
been twenty-three unauthorised encampments involving 132 caravans,
and twenty-one official (publicly-provided) and private sites on which
were stationed 483 caravans. These were concentrated in Alyn and
Deeside, Wrexham Maelor, Pembrokeshire, Merthyr Tydfil, Cardiff and
Swansea. Two trends are notable from the figures: unauthorised
encampments are, perhaps naturally, higher where there are few or no
official sites, and yet many authorities who manage no official sites also
appear to have experienced no unauthorised encampments.

In January 1997 the Welsh Office estimated that there were 846
Traveller children in Wales: 268 between the ages 0-4, 369 between 5-
10, and 209 from 11-16. The statistics are the last to be collated by the
Welsh Office. Within a few years of the coming into force of the
Criminal Justice and Public Order Act 1994, the Welsh Office decided
that the bi-annual central collection of the count of Gypsies in Wales
was no longer justified.

In July 1997 a civil servant in the Planning Division of the Welsh Office wrote:

> 'The count was a purely voluntary arrangement designed to provide the Department with the necessary background information to assess whether, in the event of a complaint, a county council had fulfilled its statutory duty ... With the repeal of the appropriate part of the 1968 legislation the need for central collection of the information ceased; although clearly there is a need for each unitary authority to collect the information – along with a host of other information that each needs for various purposes – to ensure that they are effectively implementing policies for education, public health and the like.'

In 1998 the School of Education at the University of Wales Cardiff and the Save the Children Fund (SCF) published *Traveller children and educational need in Wales*. Like the 1996 OFSTED Report in England, the SCF Report identifies far greater numbers of travelling children in Wales than official governmental counts would suggest. This can be partly be explained by the fact that only those people deemed to be Gypsies in the Romany or Traditional Traveller sense are counted by the Welsh Office (WO) while the researcher obtained information from departments other those approached by the WO and also because Traveller children may have been unrecorded in the WO counts if they went unseen. The SCF Report suggests that there are at least 1,809 Traveller children in Wales.

It is clear that official estimates of the number of Travelling people in England and Wales should be treated with distrust. They are not counted by all authorities; those that do undertake the count may not include Travelling people whom they deem not to be 'Gypsies'. Other counts by statutory and voluntary educational bodies put the numbers much higher, at double the official numbers and the figures do not, as the Government's own 1991 research recognised, say anything about the people counted or about their needs and desires. More telling is the fact that Travelling people are not included on the National Census, even within the 'Other' category of ethnic minority groups. It is equally difficult to estimate how many Travelling people are settled in housing how long they will remain there and whether they have been pushed or pulled into housing.

Gypsy Traveller Support

Cardiff Gypsy Sites Group (CGSG) is the only known Gypsy and Traveller support Group in Wales (although of course some national, British Gypsy organisations may offer support to Gypsies in Wales). England has such voluntary organisations in Avon, Buckinghamshire, Hertfordshire, London, Sheffield and York, to name but a few.

CGSG was set up in 1981, and offers an extensive advice and liaison service to the Gypsy Traveller community and all service-providing agencies in Cardiff and the surrounding area. Issues dealt with include planning, site development, grazing rights, site management, housing, homelessness, racial harassment and discrimination, health, legal matters and welfare. Welfare advice, information and offers of representation are given during scheduled drop-in office sessions, and fortnightly surgeries on one of the two official sites in Cardiff.

Five recorded cases of racial harassment of Gypsy Travellers in Cardiff occurred in 1998. The Commission for Racial Equality was helpful in resolving two of these: in one case two Gypsy Travellers were dismissed from their jobs because it was discovered that they had family on one of the sites; another involved false accusations in a large supermarket. In another case the Cardiff Mediation Service was used where a Gypsy family in housing were the subject of racial abuse from a neighbour. CGSG also arranged, with Cardiff Council, a successful Gypsy Traveller Awareness Day which was held at County Hall in October 1998.

CGSG is finding that, due to the enabling approach taken since the conception of the Group and the increased literacy and telephone ownership of site residents (and housed Gypsies) in recent years, referral work is gradually reducing. They continue to liaise with the local authority, seeking playgrounds on the two official sites (one of which is twenty years old and sited in a particularly unpleasant and sterile place) and pressing for another site. An independent consultation with Gypsy Travellers in the area identified accommodation, site safety and play space as being issues of concern.

CGSG's Annual Report for 1997/98 notes that the accommodation situation for this period is a continuing one, with a shortage of local authority site provision, no private provision and a corresponding push into housing. The Group has managed to prevent some families from having to present themselves as homeless by setting up a scheme whereby mobile homes can be privately rented from a caravan company.

Accommodation

Sadly, settled people and the print media often seem to confuse accommodation issues with criminal matters. The only real link is that, since 1994, the way of life of Gypsies and Travellers has been criminalised due to a lack of legal stopping places.

A Gypsy organisation has evidence from 1996 which shows that, on occasion, officers of the Gwent Constabulary have ignored Welsh Office Circular 76/94 (identical in content to Home Office Circular 1/94) and guidance issued by the Association of Chief Police Officers, which advises that police powers under the Criminal Justice and Public Order Act 1994 should not be used needlessly. Indeed, it appears that some officers may have approached landowners who are permitting Gypsies and Travellers to stay on their land, offering to employ their powers of eviction under Section 61.

Of course, as in England, there would be little need for powers to deal with unauthorised encampments if accommodation for Travelling people were provided or enabled as it is for settled people. Wales has a patchy history in this regard. Two authorities were criticised in judicial reviews under the Caravan Sites Act 1968 for not complying with their statutory duty to provide sites: West Glamorgan, in the 1986 case of Rafferty, and Dyfed in the 1988 case of Price.

Cardiff Gypsy Sites Group calculate that there were forty-nine roadside families on twenty-three unauthorised encampments in the Cardiff and Vale of Glamorgan area during 1997/8, approximately half of whom were in need of permanent accommodation.

The Vale of Glamorgan has seen a long-running saga in recent years, in which a Gypsy man with long-standing local connections purchased his own land but was unable to gain planning permission to live on it with his family. Instead, the local authority gave itself (deemed) planning permission of a parcel of land in their ownership, for the Gypsy family to rent as licensees, upon which nearby villagers set up a campaign against the site and sought judicial review of the local authorities' decision. The Gypsy concerned was not made a party to the legal challenge, although he clearly had a direct interest in the outcome (including the possibility of being made homeless); he successfully sought judicial review of the matter himself in order to become a party to proceedings. The matter is not yet resolved and has been ongoing since 1990.

In Wrexham, North Wales, a long struggle between local settled people and the local authority over plans for a new site did, unusually, result in the site being built. In 1996 a local resident had set up a group called CATS (Campaign Against Traveller Sites) and was running 'local democracy' meetings in a school hall until the local church complained. A number of families are now well settled on the new site or in housing – supported by local service-providers – but some families are reluctant to leave the old site upon which they have resided for some time and many problems are far from resolved. While difficult to prove, it appears that a disproportionate number of Wrexham pubs continue to illegally display 'No Travellers' signs aimed presumably at the residents of the two sites. Flintshire, too, has also successfully developed a new site in the last year or two. Of course, the flip side of such positive progress is that these authorities now appear to operate a 'zero-toleration' policy to unauthorised encampments, compelling Travelling people to leave the area or enter housing.

Housing Gypsies

Cardiff Gypsy Sites Group note that increasing numbers of young couples are forced to present themselves as homeless and move into housing as there is no alternative accommodation available to them. The relationship between Gypsies and Travellers and housing in Cardiff was explored in 1992 by Professor Phil Thomas and Sue Campbell of Cardiff Law School in the report Housing Gypsies. Thomas and Campbell spoke to Gypsies and Travellers on sites and in houses, and settled people who were local politicians or worked in a professional capacity in the accommodation field.

The research was undertaken at a time when the last Conservative government was undertaking 'consultation' on reform of the Caravan Sites Act (resulting in the Criminal Justice and Public Order Act 1994 and the repeal of the local authority duty to provide Gypsy sites). None of the Travellers interviewed had heard or been told of the proposed reforms which might have a considerable impact on their lives. When told that the measures were in part a result of a government crackdown on 'hippies' and 'ravers', many began to express antipathy to New Age Travellers; government reforms and messages seem to have deepened divisions within the travelling communities.

Paragraph 27 of the 1992 consultation paper stated: 'Gypsies may not find it easy to provide sites for themselves and, if they do manage to find a site, the process of settling down and possibly transferring into traditional housing may not be easy for people who are accustomed to a nomadic lifestyle. Accordingly, the Government believes that it may be necessary to provide advice on education, health and housing which encourages Gypsies and other travellers to settle and, in time, to transfer into traditional housing. It may also be necessary to inform public opinion about the advantages of permitting official sites and encouraging Gypsies to settle so that they become integrated into the community.'

A Cardiff Councillor said:

As far as I am concerned the Travellers are born into a way of life that they want to preserve and I do not think that they should be forced into housing. The other issue is that there aren't any houses for them to be forced into because in Cardiff there is a large waiting list. There are lots of families in B & B and where are the houses going to be found for the travellers?

A Gypsy commented that 'They would need huge houses to put us in 'cause of the size of our families. If you have five children you must have a four bedroomed house. What if you have ten or thirteen children? They'd have to knock two or three houses together.'

Another Gypsy said:

When my parents died, a house-dwelling friend took me in her house for the night but I could not sleep upstairs so I slept downstairs on a settee by a door. I like to be by a door, I can't settle unless I'm near a door.

The government proposals also suggested that, if not wanting to move into housing, Gypsies should provide their own sites for themselves. However, while many families would probably like to have their own plot, racial prejudice, inability to meet the requirements of settled money lenders, lack of financial paperwork and the need to produce a documented list of past addresses – not to mention the lack of affordable land – can all stand in the way. As one Cardiff Gypsy said, 'We tried to find land in all parts of Cardiff and we were unsuccessful. We also tried in many other parts of the country without luck. Once the owner found out we were Gypsies the deal was off.' Another said:

> even if you can afford a piece of ground you can't do what you like with it. I know some farmers very well. I could buy from them and pay so much each week but not through a bank or anything like that, but you couldn't live on it 'cos you won't get permission.

Education

In writing *Traveller children and educational need in Wales*, the SCF Report mentioned above, the researchers interviewed Travellers in Wales and ascertained that there were two major obstacles to the provision of education for Traveller children: their nomadic lifestyle and culture and the incompatibility between these and the conventional provision of education. 'A general lack of appreciation of Traveller lifestyle and culture has culminated in misunderstandings and misconceptions on all sides.' Travellers seemed keen to at least provide education for their children at a primary level but also felt that school supplied only a part of their children's education.

Some local authorities in Wales seem to refuse to acknowledge the presence of Travelling families in their areas and thereby do not meet their statutory educational duties. There also, despite the recommendations of Welsh Office Circular 52/90 on inter-agency working, appears to be little co-ordination between different departments within local authorities with regard to the provision of services to Travellers.

The findings in Wales with respect to the education of travelling children in Wales are much the same of those in the OFSTED Report on England. What is different is the level of specialist support available to the children in Wales. If 'Traveller Education Service' (TES) is defined in the English sense, as a county-wide service with a dedicated head and other specialist workers and Education Act 1996 Section 488 funding, then there is only one such service, in Cardiff. Highly effective but less well-resourced services operate in Swansea and Wrexham. Other 'services' throughout the country may only consist of a sole named person with some responsibility and who may not provide a county-wide service.

Only seven TESs in Wales receive Section 488 funding. In contrast to England, the central government contributes 75 per cent (not 65 per cent). Nevertheless, until 1998 £11.5 million was available to TESs in England but only £150,000 to Wales. According to an estimate by SCF, this means that 6 per cent of Travelling people in Britain are in Wales, but receive only 2.5.per cent of the special funding for education services. The Welsh Office recently announced that it is doubling the amount of money available for 'development work' in Traveller education. However, due to their significant under-estimate of the numbers of travelling children mentioned above, the anomaly between England and Wales will remain the same.

Research and reform

In March 1995 the Telephone Legal Advice Service for Travellers (TLAST) was set up in Cardiff Law School at the University of Wales and ran for three years. TLAST provided advice and referral (legal and practical) for Travelling people in England and Wales who, due to their lifestyle, face particular legal problems exacerbated by the inaccessibility of legal services. The often isolated locations of Travellers make access to specialist legal advice by telephone more user-friendly, due to the increased use of mobile telephones amongst the Traveller community.

The work of TLAST had the following aims:

1. To provide a front-line telephone legal advice service for Travellers.
2. To encourage best practice through the development of a referral/liaison network amongst specialist legal practitioners (around 100) willing to undertake Traveller-related casework from first enquiry through to test cases in the UK and Europe where appropriate.
3. To undertake and disseminate research about the legal needs of Travellers in order to inform the future policy of organisations dealing with publicly funded legal services.

There were over 1,200 calls made to the service by Travelling people themselves and those working for and on behalf of Gypsies and Travellers in their professional capacity. The highest number of calls related to problems obtaining planning permission to develop privately owned land, and legal problems relating to unauthorised encampments; there were also many calls regarding discrimination and racial harassment experienced by Gypsies and Travellers on private and public sites and in housing.

In March, 1997 TLAST organised a conference with specialist speakers from the Republic of Ireland, Scotland, Northern Ireland, England and Wales which aimed to provide a forum at which imaginative and practical proposals for Traveller law reform could be raised. The conference was attended by more than ninety Traveller-related organisations including local authority personnel, teachers of Travellers, health visitors, legal practitioners, planners, church officers, police officers and individuals. Emerging from the conference were proposals for the development of specialist Traveller Working Groups (TWiGs), which began to meet in March 1998 with a view to providing a common platform to lobby for Traveller law reform.

TLAST concluded in April 1998 but the Traveller Law Research Unit (TLRU) of which it was a part continues to exist and to facilitate a platform for Traveller law reform. Following six months of meetings with the TWiGs, discussing accommodation and site provision, eviction and criminal justice, planning, education, and health and social services, in London in February 1999 TLRU ran a second conference on Traveller law reform. This brought together nearly 200 people and organisations, including Travelling people and government representatives, to discuss and agree practical, imaginative and realisable reform proposals in the law, policy and practice affecting Gypsies and Travellers. The report of the TWiGs and the papers given at the conference were edited by the TLRU and published in May as *Gaining Ground: Law Reform for Gypsies and Travellers* with the launch being hosted by Lord Avebury in the House of Lords. It is hoped that a momentum towards reform has been created and can be sustained.

The Future

The law for Gypsies and other Travelling people, in Wales as in England, needs to be created and/or amended so that two principles can be honoured:

* The way of life of Travelling people is legal and legitimate, and should be respected and enabled.
• Gypsies and other Travelling people, including those in housing, while respected for their 'differentness', must be treated equally with settled people. This may entail providing the same services as are provided for settled people but using a more culturally appropriate method of service delivery.

It is difficult to know what will happen when the Welsh National Assembly commences its governance. While the two men who have leading roles in the Assembly following devolution both have professional experience with and are sympathetic to Gypsy and Traveller issues (indeed, one has Gypsy connections by marriage), it remains to be seen whether a new Assembly will find the time or the will to tackle some of the problems faced by Gypsies and Travellers in Wales.

3

Scotland

Scottish Travellers

> 'Literally gallons of ink have been utilised developing theories as to the origin of these people [Scottish Travellers]. It would seem to me to be an exercise in futility to review all of these and even more to attempt to justify any of them. Their origin is lost in the far past and can hardly be reconstructed.'

Whilst agreeing with the words of social anthropologist Farnham Rehfisch in the above passage, it is possible to sketch a probable history of the Scottish Travellers. However, we must acknowledge his point about reconstructing the past when it comes to the question of origins and our contemporary interpretation and reading of ancient historical documents. What follows below is an attempt to offer some insight into the origins, history and contemporary situation of the Nachins or Travellers in Scotland.

Numbers

The authors' estimation of the Traveller population of Scotland in the late 1990s is around the 23,000 mark. This figure is derived from a mixture of official Scottish Office statistics (1992) and various other sources (such as the Scottish Gypsy-Traveller Association and the Save the Children Fund in Scotland). This figure of 23,000 includes Irish Travellers, Romany chals, Border Gypsies, Welsh Kalé Romanies and New Travellers (see Chapter 1 for full details). We estimate that Scottish

Travellers themselves constitute at least 7,000 people living in caravans and another 8,000 living in houses. However, Timothy Neat (1998) in his recent book *The Summer Walkers* estimates a Scottish Traveller population alone of over 20,000 with about a quarter of this figure still travelling. Whatever the accurate figure is, it is not so much numbers that are important than the nature of the contemporary relationship between settled Scottish society and one of its oldest indigenous ethnic minority groups: the *Nachins*.

The official counts

In the thirty years up to July 1998, when the new bi-annual count system was introduced, there had only ever been two official (that is central government-sponsored) counts of Travellers in Scotland. The first was in 1969 where 450 households of Scottish Travellers containing 2,100 persons were counted. The second count was conducted in 1992 by the Scottish Office census team and this indicated between 750-800 Traveller households in Scotland. Estimates of New Traveller families in Scotland vary wildly but the 1992 count put the figure at fifty. Whilst the Department of the Environment has conducted counts twice a year (in January and July) in England for quite some time, Scotland has only just introduced this system. Clearly the previous situation was not good enough to give us an accurate picture of what were the numbers, situation and circumstances of Scottish Travellers. Although it is admirable that the Scottish Office has introduced the bi-annual count at long last, it still has many question marks over its accuracy and methodology.

It was not just the infrequency issue that was the problem. When the report of the 1992 count was published it was harshly criticised by a variety of organisations. For example, Save the Children Fund (SCF) suggested at least four major problems with the methodology employed for the study. These included the timing and staffing of the count. The survey period was a two-week period in March and April rather than following the English model of taking two census counts during a twelve month period to take account of seasonal variations and travel patterns. Likewise, the staffing issue was a concern as the count was conducted by volunteer health visitors in addition to their normal duties and workloads. SCF felt that a dedicated full-time team of counters should have been employed to undertake the survey. Indeed, for the July 1998 count it was site managers and the police who were largely relied upon by the Scottish Office for the collection of data. The third criticism of the survey was that it did not take into account those Scottish Travellers who had moved into settled housing during the intervening twenty-three years between counts. Again, this was seen as a problem with the recent July 1998 count. It is clear that, for many Travellers, their lifestyle, in particular relating to work, is still maintained even for those Travellers who live in houses for all or at least part of the year. The other main complaint was the fact that the count did not utilise the local knowledge of Travellers themselves in identifying local authority and roadside sites, some of which are in remote or isolated locations. This was considered to be a glaring omission and methodological problem for the count. Those Travellers who were parked-up in out of the way places were missed by the health visitors when other Travellers may well have had the information to locate certain sites and encampments. The numbers collected during such counts is very important as they are used by the Scottish Office to help inform pitch targets and the Toleration Policy.

Origins

According to some sources, Travelling people in Scotland can trace their roots back as far as the Twelfth century. The Farandman laws, which existed at the time, identified a group known as 'tinklers' and gave them some degree of legal protection 'to go about their business'. Other evidence illustrates that such 'tinklers' were highly skilled travelling silversmiths and metalworkers who were employed by the various clans and clan chiefs to manufacture weapons and other such goods. Their status was relatively high and they were regarded as being nomadic artisans with much to offer potential employers.

Today, many Scottish Travellers claim roots that pre-date even these written records. They see themselves as the proud forebears of a tradition and culture which can be traced back to the nomadic hunter gatherers of ancient Scotland.

It seems clear then that there were nomadic Travellers in Scotland prior to the Romanies arriving from about 1500 onwards. It is therefore uncertain whether or not records in the Middle Ages refer to indigenous Scottish Travellers or Romany Gypsies. What is very clear is that over the centuries the two groups have intermarried and the present-day population of Scottish Travellers is of mixed descent. In their own language of Cant they call themselves *Nachins* (or *Nawkens*). The Cant has a huge and exotic vocabulary of words which are derived from a variety of different sources. In the north east of Scotland the Cant has a Gaelic structure whilst in the South, around the borders, it is a version of Romani with English (known as *poggerdi chib* to English Romany chals). Scottish Travellers have a rich history and a tradition of artistic endeavours. Many ballads have been preserved from the Scottish tradition by Travellers such as the Stewart family. Likewise, folk-story tellers such as Duncan Williamson and Jimmy McBeath have written books which keep alive the history, values and traditions of Scottish Travellers. During the summer months some families make a living from piping in Glencoe and other attractive tourist destinations in Scotland.

Under James IV and V

Written records from 1491 indicate that 'Spaniards' danced before the Scottish King on the streets of Edinburgh. These 'Spaniards' may or may not have been Romanies – the evidence is somewhat inconclusive. However, in 1505 a small group of Romany Gypsies certainly arrived – possibly from Spain – saying they were pilgrims and James IV granted them an audience and provided them with some money. They were later sent to Scandinavia (Denmark in fact) with a letter of recommendation. A second group of dancers from Spain in 1529 were undoubtedly Romanies and they performed for James V. A record dating from 1540 shows that James V granted this group the autonomy to pass their own laws and adhere to their own customs under John Faw, 'Duke of little Egypt'. However, a year later this decree was repealed and all Gypsies were ordered to leave Scotland. This rapid change of policy allegedly came about due to the fact that James V had been in a fight with three Gypsies. The king was well known for travelling around Scotland in disguise. James died in 1542 and so the new law was not enacted and a year later John Faw was again officially known to be in charge of the Scottish Gypsies.

Persecution and discrimination

In 1573 a new law was passed which had severe implications for Gypsies in Scotland at that time. It stated that Gypsies had to either leave the country or sedentarise and hold down paid employment. The penalty for Gypsies not complying with this new law was extremely harsh: imprisonment, public whipping and deportation from the realm. Incredibly, the following year saw an increase in the powers of this 1573 law and Gypsies could now be whipped and branded if they did not comply with the law on settlement and wage labour. In the borders, a popular punishment for female Gypsies in particular – for the slightest misdemeanour – was the removal of the ears. Those Gypsies who did remain in the locality and refused to settle were put to death. In 1597 other punishments was added to the growing list of sanctions used against nomadic Gypsies in Scotland: forced labour and banishment for life.

The Seventeenth century saw further state action against Gypsies, and also those who aided and abetted them. For example, one record from 1608 shows that two Scots were fined for selling food and drink to Gypsies. Noblemen who protected Gypsies on their estates were also fined for 'harbouring' them on Scottish soil. Executions of Gypsies, in the form of public hangings, were frequently recorded in the early part of the Seventeenth century in Scotland. Later in this period banishment was commonly used and one record from 1665 shows a shipping company obtaining permission from the King to send Gypsies abroad.

The year 1707 was significant, as this was when the Scottish Parliament was dissolved and future legislation was made in Westminster. In the years following this event, existing Scottish anti-Gypsy Acts continued to be applied. For example, in 1774 two female Gypsies were executed and ten Gypsies were deported from Scotland to Virginia.

Later in the century came the bloody defeat of the Jacobite uprising in 1745 and the final destruction of the ancient clan system soon after. These events led to many people being regarded as rebels and they were forced to flee their local area. Such people took to the road adding to the numbers of those already leading a nomadic way of life. Likewise, the

Highland clearances also led to a situation where some families were dispossessed and forced on to the road.

The Trespass Act of 1865

One of the most significant pieces of legislation that has, and still is, being used against Travellers in Scotland is the Trespass (Scotland) Act of 1865. This Act was introduced to control the movement of indigenous Scottish Travellers and indeed the police still regularly use this legislation today to move Travellers on from stopping places rather than use the newer but more cumbersome sections of the Criminal Justice and Public Order Act 1994.

The Advisory Committee

It is interesting to note that the Caravan Sites Act of 1968, which led to the creation of Local Authority sites, only ever applied to England and Wales. Scotland has a different system altogether. This is, of course, due to Scotland's separate legal identity and governmental devolution. In place of the clearer statutory framework that existed under the 1968 Act, the Scottish Office, in 1971, established an Advisory Committee on Scotland's Travelling People which has been renewed at intervals for three year periods. The membership of the Committee included some limited representation of Travellers. The eighth of its regular reports, covering the period 1995-7, has recently been completed and published. The Advisory Committee has the job of encouraging Scottish local authorities to build caravan sites for their indigenous Traveller population and the smaller groups of Irish Travellers as well as Welsh and English Romany chals who visit the country regularly for economic reasons.

Local authority sites

When the Advisory Committee was first established, grant aid for the establishment of Traveller sites was offered at a level of 75 per cent for building costs under the terms of the Countryside (Scotland) Act 1967. Following a slow take up of such grants, a 100 per cent grant was introduced in 1980 and this operated until 1996. The 100 per cent grant was then extended for a further two years and in December 1998 it came to an end for good. It does not appear likely, at the time of writing, that this grant will be re-introduced in the future.

The provision of local authority sites has steadily increased over the last two decades and there are now thirty-two sites available throughout the year and three that open on a seasonal basis (Banff, Innerleithen and Newtownmore). The location of sites, although they are relatively evenly spread throughout most of Scotland, does leave a lot to be desired in some parts of the country. For example, the Borders and Dumfries and Galloway in particular have far fewer sites and pitches than are required. Indeed, there is no public site provision north of Inverness at all and no provision from October through to April in the Borders. It should be noted as well that not all Scottish Travellers like, use or can even gain access to local authority sites. Such sites are criticised by Travellers as having too many cumbersome rules and regulations to meet. For example, it is suggested that there is an unnecessary amount of detail required from an individual when completing an application form for a pitch on a site when compared with the information required of someone who is applying for a council house (e.g., National Insurance number, car or van registration number, etc.). Also, many Travellers point to the fact that sites are too uniform and restrictive in their design, giving no consideration for workspace or play areas for children. Other questions have arisen concerning the keeping of pets and restrictions on visitors. The recent Douglas Report (see below) did illustrate the discretion that site managers have in letting pitches and this can be open to a level of influence that would be totally unacceptable in the allocation of council housing.

Likewise, an important issue related to pitch provision on local authority sites in Scotland is the rent factor. In 1995 the Scottish Office commissioned a 'provider' survey of all local authorities with Traveller sites. The Anne Douglas Consultancy report was published in May 1997 and was based on in-depth interviews with site managers and local authority staff (but not residents). The report covers a variety of areas but the rents issue is one that is worthy of some attention here. The Douglas Report found that the average pitch rent for a site in Scotland was £36.42 (ranging from £18.13 to £54.60). When compared with the average council house rent of £31.87 (ranging from £23.20 to £42.00) it seems that Travellers in Scotland are paying a high price for this particular mode of accommodation. Following the publication of the report, the Advisory Committee did write to all local authorities reminding them of the need to fix prices at a level which will not only ensure high occupancy sites but also take into account their council house rents. It is unknown whether or not local authority pitch rents have been reduced following this communication from the Advisory Committee. The question must be asked, although, given that until recently local authorities received a 100 per cent grant from central government to develop and build their sites, why are rents so high?

Following the reorganisation of local government in 1996, the Advisory Committee reviewed the earlier pitch target figures and concluded that the target should increase from 939 to 941. More recently the target number has come down to 927. The situation as of February 1997 showed that 543 pitches had been provided by local authorities, this meaning a shortfall of some 384 pitches. However, it should be noted that the numerical principles of pitch targets in Scotland have remained virtually unchanged for nearly two decades and have not increased to reflect household growth during this period. Those local authorities that have insufficient pitches to meet demand in their area are asked to operate a 'Toleration Policy' to illegally parked caravans. This policy does not apply in situations where twelve or more caravans are camped in one place, a higher figure than that set by the Criminal Justice and Public Order Act 1994. There are other issues which cause concern regarding the Toleration Policy however. In Ireland, which operates a similar kind of Toleration Policy to that followed in Scotland, critics have spoken of it being akin to a form of 'racialised internal immigration policy' rather than a 'Toleration Policy'. Similarly, the Scottish policy has no legal weight, is not monitored in any way and is often, according to some reports, ignored without fear of penalty.

Access to caravan sites

Private sites in Scotland are included in the national pitch target set by the Scottish Office and some organisations working with Travellers in Scotland have noted the difficulty that Travellers have in gaining access to such sites. For this reason, Save the Children undertook a project in June and September 1997 to investigate the situation. The SCF Traveller Section for Scotland conducted a small research study which aimed to establish whether or not private and council caravan sites in Scotland were discriminating against renting pitches to Scottish Travellers and Gypsies. A total of forty-three caravan sites were visited, eight of these were local authority owned and the remaining thirty-five were private. The research covered a large area of Scotland, from the Borders to the Highlands. The findings of the study were very clear: for example, 63 per cent of requests for accommodation from Travellers were refused and 50 per cent of caravan parks owned by local authorities refused entry to Travellers despite pitches being available. Indeed, some sites had signs displayed to this effect: 'SORRY - NO TRAVELLING PEO-PLE OR COMMERCIAL VEHICLES. NO TRADERS'. The SCF research report lists eight main recommendations which include the Scottish Office urgently revising their data and information on non local authority caravan parks and further investigations from the Commission for Racial Equality.

The Criminal Justice and Public Order Act (1994)

In November 1994 the Criminal Justice and Public Order Act (CJPOA) was introduced. This Act, unlike the Caravan Sites Act 1968, applied in Scotland as well as England and Wales. This legislation was largely a result of the very public conflict in England between landowners, local authorities, the police and New Travellers. The result of the CJPOA has been to effectively criminalise a nomadic lifestyle. Some writers have referred to the Act as a form of 'ethnic cleansing' and in a sense they are quite right. To criminalise nomadism is a specific form of forced cultural assimilation for Travellers. The pressure is now on Gypsies and other Travellers to stop travelling as to park a caravan for even the shortest of periods on once traditional roadside sites can be a criminal (not civil) offence and risks having your caravan, i.e. your home, impounded, as well as fines and prison sentences. Such pressures as this, and various other pieces of civil and criminal legislation in Scotland, have made things much more difficult for Scottish Traveller families attempting to

Notice barring Travellers (and contractors) from this private site in Scotland;
photograph by Michelle Lloyd, Save the Children Fund.

Site blocked by a local Council in Scotland; *photograph by Michelle Lloyd, Save the Children Fund.*

access public services such as local schools, libraries and health services. A research study has recently started at Dundee University (in association with Save the Children Fund) to establish the social and legal effects of families being 'moved on' so regularly.

Health

With constant evictions and being told to 'move on', access to good health services is still difficult for many Travellers in Scotland. The hardships of a Traveller lifestyle are reflected in the general health of the population. Such traditional indicators as infant mortality and life expectancy rates reflect the nature of life continually on the move.

For those Travellers on local authority sites, being registered with a local General Practitioner can still be something of a problem. This is especially true for those who do not live on a local authority site; registering and obtaining treatment from a GP can be problematic. One of the main issues for Travellers in this situation is the lack of access to preventative treatments and screening programmes such as cervical and breast cancer. Similarly, according to research from England, programmes dealing with the immunisation of children have a low take-up in comparison with the settled population. This is due to a number of complicated factors, not all of which reflect Traveller lifestyle and cultural beliefs. Wider environmental factors play a crucial role in determining one's health and the recent study by Save the Children Fund in Scotland, The Right to Roam, found that local authority sites were likely to have three or more hazards (such as electricity pylons, landfill tips, canals and the like) when compared with private ones.

Travellers in Scotland, like their counterparts in England and Wales, take a pragmatic attitude to their health, that is they tend to seek out direct help only when the immediate need arises. For example, the use of hospital accident and emergency (A&E) departments is quite popular amongst many Travellers close to urban areas. Of course, there are other reasons why Travellers use A&E departments. If a GP refuses to do a site or camp visit then quite often there is no choice but to use these facilities.

Like many other central and local government departments which rely on a fixed address for keeping in contact with people, health authorities do face difficulties in maintaining contact with Traveller patients and keeping their medical records up to date and in the right location. It seems clear that to resolve this problematic issue departments will need to devise a national strategy and system which does not just rely on individual goodwill and a fixed address to keep in contact with patients. Many innovative projects for keeping links with patients who move, like the one being run by Argyll doctor Iain McNicol, are now being developed and could be one step in the right direction.

The Secretary of State's Advisory Committee on Scotland's Travelling People, in their eighth term report published in 1998, gave little attention to the health needs of Scottish Travellers admitting that 'there is little evidence available to the Advisory Committee regarding the state of Travelling People's health.' This is a view shared by the Save the Children Traveller project based in Edinburgh. In a recent 'Poverty Briefing' Report SCF recognised that 'there are few studies on the health needs of Travelling People and most relate to areas outwith Scotland'.

One of the few studies that has been published relating to the health needs of Scottish Travellers dates back to 1992 and was undertaken by the Scottish Association of Health Councils. In this report a number of problems were documented, including: difficulties in obtaining access to primary medical care as some GPs are unwilling to register temporary patients; poor access to screening and immunisation; poor continuity of care and record keeping; evictions soon after birth and lack of access to ante-natal and community midwives.

For many Scottish Travellers long-term health education and preventative medicine come as a secondary concern to the rather more pressing matters of finding a suitable and safe stopping place for their trailer and finding the next bit of work.

Work

Just like Gypsies and Travellers in England and Wales, it is a clear preference of Scottish Travellers to work for themselves using many skills in a variety of occupations. The family as an economic unit is all important and the concept of retirement is largely unknown. The pursuit of independent or casual employment takes many forms. Trades include scrap dealing, tarmac'ing, agricultural work, carpet or furniture dealing, gardening work and many others such as dealing in used cars. Horse trading still occurs at the various fairs (see box below) and is symbolically important. One occupation that some Scottish Travellers engage in is collecting whelks and 'pearl fishing' on the east and west coasts of the Highlands. It is clear when looking at the history of Scottish Travellers and their relationship with work that when some markets contract (e.g., tinsmithing, agricultural work), Travellers will adapt and find new markets that are expanding, such as carpet or furniture dealing.

Writing in 1975, Farnham Rehfisch noted that Scottish Travellers' attitude towards steady employment was coloured by a number of factors. The first was that employment would almost invariably put them in a position of inferiority vis-à-vis members of the Flatties. Secondly, few Travellers had very much formal education, hence they are eligible only for menial jobs. In competition with Flatties they would not show to advantage, and so their self-image would be challenged. The absence of need for steady employment was taken as evidence that members of the group are cleverer than others at earning, hence to take a regular job would be an admission of failure.

Many things have changed since Rehfisch made these observations but the principles of nomadism, self-employment, adaptability, flexibility and knowledge of a multitude of trades has not changed for Scottish Travellers' relationship to work.

As in other areas of Scottish Traveller life, the division of labour regarding income is marked. The men are generally in charge of things like organising transport whilst the women are largely in charge of the domestic chores. Both, however, contribute in different ways to the 'family purse'. The occupations listed above are generally male ones whilst women will contribute to the household income via trades such as running a market stall, selling bedding and towels, hawking and collecting old clothes from door-to-door in Flattie housing estates.

The image of Scottish Traveller work is still bound up in notions of selling 'lucky white heather', clothes pegs and conducting fortune-telling at fairs and shows. Perhaps because of this there is a tendency to see Traveller occupations as being somehow out of date, historical and static. However, it can be seen that the Traveller population in Scotland continues to exist, grow and be successful in the economic sphere. This

Summer Camp, Norfolk.
Many Nawkens travel South in the Summer to visit settled relatives attracted by the possibility of work; *photograph by David Gallant.*

is the other side of 'Traveller poverty' which is often the only side of the story that we hear about. To be clear, not all Scottish Travellers are poor, downtrodden, welfare-dependent and living in squalor – far from it.

This success in the economic sphere is a direct result of the many skills that Travellers have in generating an income and taking advantage of new economic opportunities that come along. It is only through this quick adaptation to new market opportunities that the Traveller economy develops and flourishes. The best example here is what we now call 'recycling': Travellers can with some justification claim to be amongst the first 'greens' on the planet. Their productive economic future seems assured rather than in jeopardy.

Scottish horse fairs

Still going:
St Boswells, Borders, 17-19 July*
Aikey Brae, Aberdeenshire, 22 July*
Brechin, Angus, July
Kelso, Borders, 26 July

Closed:
Musselburgh, East Lothian, 2nd week in August (closed 1996)
Falkirk Tryst, Falkirk, 2nd week in September (closed in the 1980s)
Kirk Yetholm, Borders, August (closed in the 1930s)

English fairs which Scottish Travellers traditionally attended:
Appleby, Cumbria, 1st Wednesday in June
Epsom Downs, Derby
Broughhill, near Appleby, 30th September – 1st October

Closed:
Doncaster, St Leger, September

* These are currently under serious threat of closure.

Education

Scottish Travellers who are parents are increasingly accepting the importance of literacy and state education. Many make regular use of local primary schools and choose those where they feel their children will be welcomed and have a positive learning experience.

All local authorities in Scotland (and indeed the rest of Britain) have a statutory duty to provide an 'adequate and efficient' education for all children in their area and operate equal opportunities polices.However it is still the case that some schools in certain parts of the country are unable or unwilling to meet the needs of Traveller children. Reasons given by schools vary but the main ones seem to centre around real or perceived problems relating to the extra time required and the organisational adjustments that have to be made in order to accommodate small numbers of Travellers for what may be a very brief period. Added to this the problems encountered by Traveller children when they do actually manage to attend school (e.g. racism, bullying and exclusion) make future non-attendance a real possibility. Negative messages about their experience of school are passed on to younger members of the family so that some children may never actually be enrolled at any school.

Obviously, take up of school places requires a degree of permanent residence and with the passing of the Criminal Justice and Public Order Act in 1994 and the misapplication of the Toleration Policy this has become much more difficult to achieve for those on roadside sites. In these circumstances, and with a lack in Scotland of externally targeted staff for Travellers, anything other than sporadic attendance at a variety of different schools is a real problem for some children.

It is still true today that many Traveller children do not go on to secondary schooling after completing primary school. According to *The Right to roam* by Save The Children Fund, only 41 per cent of those Traveller children interviewed said they attended primary school with any degree of regularity. At secondary school this figure went down to a fifth. University or college attendance is rarer still, although there are exceptions to this generalisation. This means that after the age of eleven or twelve, a 'Traveller education' is seen as important to the children's future roles and careers as Travellers. Without formal education, such roles take on quite a rigid sexual division of labour: the boys will enter the outside world of paid work and accompany their fathers, older brothers, uncles and cousins to learn the ropes of various trades and occupations. The girls will largely remain in the home environment and work (unpaid) alongside their mothers and older sisters, learning the skills required to attend to the home and children. Teenage girls will also go out hawking with their mothers when required to. However, when there has been a successful integration into schooling, even on a part-time basis, young female Travellers are now participating more fully in the ordinary worlds of paid work. Some Traveller adult females have attended Access courses and other adult learning opportunities in order to run their own businesses.

The 1982 third term report of the Secretary of State's Advisory Committee devoted a full chapter to the particular educational needs of

Travellers. This seminal document, which preceded an EC Resolution on Education for Gypsies and Travellers by a full seven years, drew attention to the need for urgent concerted action at local authority and national level in order to redress the discriminatory situation which they experienced. One outcome of this report was the establishment of a funded half-time post at Moray House College of Education to set up working parties to try to develop appropriate curricular responses. This was later developed in 1990 to the creation of a National Centre, the Scottish Traveller Education Programme (STEP), with a remit to promote policy and practice in state education to support Travellers' lifestyles and cultures. With the recent integration of Moray House into the Faculty of Education at the University of Edinburgh there is a concern that the funding for STEP should continue to be protected so that the national work of the Centre can continue.

The sixth, seventh and eighth term reports of The Secretary of State's Advisory Committee on Scotland's Travelling People have noted the successes of this project, in particular the modest successes in encouraging Traveller children to continue school beyond primary age. However, they also note in the eighth term report, which has a full chapter on the particular educational needs of Travellers, the need for continuity and some potential problems that the STEP might face in terms of future funding due to changes in Higher Education. Recommendation number 23 in the eighth term report asks that:

> Given the value of the Scottish Traveller Education Programme, The Scottish Office, as a matter of urgency, takes positive action to ensure that this accumulated experience and expertise is preserved and developed as a national resource.

In another initiative, the National Lottery Charities Board has given £175,000 to the Aberdeen-based Travellers Education Project, dedicated to helping travelling people aged between twelve and twenty-five.

The eighth term report of the Advisory Committee is worth noting in relation to Traveller Education in Scotland. The report devotes a whole section (14 pages) to 'Travellers and Education'. Unlike other important issues affecting the Traveller community (such as racial discrimination, health needs and local authority pitch rents, etc.), it was not subsumed under the section entitled 'Responding to the wider needs of

Travellers'. This illustrates the political importance given to the issue of Traveller education and also the European Union interest in this issue. However, it has to be said that funding for Traveller education in Scotland has yet to match the political importance attached to it. Amongst the issues highlighted for attention in the report are: equal educational opportunities and positive discrimination for Travellers within education; vocational education; a national resource centre for Traveller education; open and distance learning as a support for mobility; exclusion problems; discrimination in schools; funding problems and many others.

The current moves towards devolution, together with an educational policy which promotes and funds a range of actions to combat social exclusion, raise achievement, reducing absenteeism and a recognition of the needs of a diverse school population, augur well for the continuance of targeted action for Travellers.

Self-representation

The Scottish Gypsy/Traveller Association (SGTA) was founded in 1993 by a group of concerned Scottish Travellers. Its aims are to give an active voice and a platform for all Travellers in Scotland, to campaign for their culture, civil rights and justice. It has organised a number of conferences and publishes an occasional magazine, *Nachin News*. Although its membership is largely concentrated in the south-east of Scotland, the SGTA has the potential to gain national status in Scotland and actively lobby local authorities and the Scottish Office on a number of issues of concern to the Scottish Traveller community. Indeed, the Scottish Office Advisory Committee has met with the executive committee of the SGTA on at least four occasions since 1993, discussing a number of issues from pitch targets to children's playgrounds. Equally, however, there have been numerous occasions where the Advisory Committee has refused to get involved or meet with the SGTA for various reasons.

A recent development in this area has been the new Scottish Traveller Consortium. This is a joint initiative between SGTA, the Scottish Human Rights Centre and SCF and has three years funding from the National Lottery (1999-2002).

It should also be remembered that a number of individual Travellers and families in Scotland speak out and challenge the prejudice they encounter on a daily basis. They will regularly participate in 'awareness-raising' training seminars and get involved in liaison meetings and the like. The voice of the individual Traveller should not be forgotten in the struggle for equality and justice.

The future

As mentioned earlier, in December 1998 the Scottish Office Development Department's grant scheme ended. This allowed local authorities to apply for grants to provide or upgrade sites for Travellers. The effects of its loss can only be speculated on at this time but it seems likely that it will have a significant impact on not only new sites being built but existing sites being upgraded and maintained.

One initiative that is being currently developed is the creation of transit sites for Travellers on farm land. The response of landowners to the Advisory Committee's Farm Sites Initiative has so far, in the committee's own words, been 'disappointing'. This is despite the availability of European Union grants to 'compensate' farmers and other landowners who take land out of agricultural production. Many Travellers, who for years have been asking for transit sites in Scotland, feel that this latest farmland initiative is bogus and not being promoted seriously. It seems clear that in Scotland, just as in England, the emphasis now will be on Traveller self-help and private provision, even though the planning system does not help this process.

Recommendation number 32, the last one made by the eighth term Advisory Committee in its report, was that The Secretary of State for Scotland 'appoint a ninth Advisory Committee to complete outstanding work'. Whilst the eighth term report makes it quite clear that a ninth term Advisory Committee must not be assumed to automatically follow, it would be a major surprise if a ninth was not appointed, considering the 'outstanding work' still to be done. However, at the same time as recommending a ninth Committee, the eighth term Committee recognises that the role and purpose of such an Advisory Committee is, apparently, close to being served. The Committee, by way of a conclusion in their report stated that:

> The Committee looks forward to completion of the site network, cou-
> pled with increased readiness on the part of both Traveller and settled
> communities to recognise and adapt successfully to each others' needs,
> aspirations and constraints.

However, for many Travellers, as well as groups and individuals working with Travellers in Scotland, this is a somewhat optimistic and one-sided assessment of what the future might hold. Many probing and critical questions have been raised by organisations like the SGTA and SCF in Scotland regarding the fundamental nature of the Advisory Committee.

They ask questions such as:

- why does it have such a limited remit?
- why is it so unrepresentative in terms of its membership?
- why does it lack accountability for its decisions and actions?
- why is there little in the way of meaningful consultation with other interested parties working with Scottish Travellers?

All these questions, and the many others like them, deserve some attention and it is hoped that if a ninth term Committee is appointed in Scotland that it may address some of these probing questions. As with Wales, it is too early to say what the future holds for Scottish Travellers in relation to the new Scottish Parliament. That story will unfold and no doubt be told in the years to come.

4

Gypsies and race relations – theory and practice

Romanies and other ethnic minorities

Since their arrival in Europe, Romanies, as well as other minorities, have often faced persecution. Arriving later than the Jews, the Romanies could not be accused, as were the former, of spreading the Black Death, although they were wrongly blamed for an outbreak of cholera in Italy as recently as 1910.

It has been said that the Romanies were 'the first Blacks in Europe'. The Romanies, dark-skinned as they were, aroused colour prejudice towards people with skins other than pink. In Romania and other parts of the Balkans they were forced into serfdom in their hundreds under rules more severe than for the local feudal serfs. They could be bought and sold, families were split up, while runaways were tortured if recaptured just as the black slaves in the Americas. The Romany serfs in Romania were not emancipated until the nineteenth century.

In Spain, expulsion orders were issued almost simultaneously against Romanies, Jews and Moors. In England, Queen Elizabeth acted against 'Blackamoors' and 'Egyptians', declaring that the former 'shall with all speed be avoided and discharged out of this her Majesty's dominions'. As for the latter, she added the death penalty for Gypsies who disobeyed an earlier order to leave the country, at the same time as she executed her doctor, the only Jew left in London after an earlier expulsion.

Many Gypsies remained, as they had nowhere else to go; some found safety by working for nobles and landowners but others were arrested and executed. York, scene of the death of forty Jews in the thirteenth century, was to witness a mass execution of Gypsies in 1596. Gypsies, however, through their nomadism were able to survive in a Britain where the forces of law were not nationally organised.

At the end of the nineteenth century Jewish and Gypsy immigrants arrived from Eastern Europe. In 1906 Major Gordon Evans spoke against German Gypsies who were trying to settle in England. He was the same MP who had organised opposition to Jewish immigration the previous year, culminating in the Aliens Act.

It is not surprising that Zionism has its echo amongst the Romanies, giving impetus to the idea of 'Romanestan', a Romany national home. Janusz Kwiek, leader of the Coppersmith tribes in Poland before 1939 came to London and spoke in Hyde Park to seek support for his proposals for a homeland in Africa. After 1945, Vaida Voevod (see below) wrote to the United Nations asking for help in getting land in India. However most Romanies have dropped the idea of a geographical nation state. Feeling like the poet Ronnie Lee who wrote: "Romanestan is where my two feet stand", they try to keep an independent cultural existence in the various countries where they live.

For the Nazis in Germany, Jews, Romanies and 'Negroes' were the only 'foreign' element in the state. For the extreme right in Britain today, all 'non-Aryans' are enemies, although anti-Semitism is less open.

Romanies are a race

The Court of Appeal in 1988 confirmed that 'Gypsies', in the original sense of Romanies, are legally recognised in Britain as an ethnic group (under the terms of the 1976 Race Relations Act). The judgement arose from a court case in which the Commission for Racial Equality (CRE) accused Mr Dutton, a publican in East London, of discrimination because he had put a notice outside his pub reading 'No travellers served'.

The CRE maintained that Travellers was a synonym for Gypsies and the notice therefore discriminated against Romanies who are a racial group within the Gypsy community. The Appeal Court ruled that Gypsies are indeed an ethnic group. Because they have a common history, culture, oral literature and practices of a religious nature they fit the so-called Mandla criteria (established in the House of Lords when it was decided that Sikhs were an ethnic group). Unlike the Saxons and the Vikings they have not been absorbed into the English nation. As the Court stated:

> On the evidence, it was clear that Gypsies in the primary sense of the word i.e. Romanies, were a minority with a long shared history and a common geographical origin. They had distinctive customs, a language derived from Romani and a common culture. Many of them had retained a separateness and self-awareness of still being Gypsies (and) had not been absorbed into the population.

This gives Gypsies protection under the 1976 Race Relations Act and the provisions against incitement to racial harassment of the Public Order Act. A notice reading 'No Gypsies served' is discriminatory. However, the Appeal Court, disagreeing with the CRE, held that the word 'Traveller' was not a synonym of 'Gypsy' but referred to a wider group, including non-Romany Travellers and 'New Age Gypsies'. They did not accept the CRE's argument that this wider group was itself an ethnic group within the Mandla criteria. A notice 'No Travellers served' is – in law – indirectly discriminatory against Romanies but it is not illegal if some justification can be given for refusing to serve Travellers as a whole (for example, 'damage to property').

The roots of prejudice

From the time of their first appearance in Britain in the early 1500s, Romanies can be compared with modern immigrants from East Africa and Asia. They came in small family groups seeking opportunities to carry on existing trades and occupations among settled populations. Little free land was available and they had no chance to establish, even if they had wanted to, their own settlements and homeland as, for example, the Vikings had done before them. Every territory had already been allocated to a nobleman or city dwelling merchant. The only place for the Romanies was, therefore, on the fringes of society where they had to make a living as best as they could. The fact that they were nomads, travelling with carts and tents, had its advantages and disadvantages. They could move to seek new markets and to avoid trouble but they did not stay in any one place long enough to build up a relationship with the local people. For centuries the nomadic lifestyle of the Romanies has been one reason why they are met with suspicion and dislike (tinged perhaps with fear and envy).

Stereotypes

Stereotyped images of the Romanies have appeared throughout their history. They provide the basis for persecution and serve to rationalise the measures taken against them. Since their arrival in Europe, Romanies have suffered particularly from two contradictory false images. The image of the mysterious and attractive wanderer, the romantic violin-playing lover or the seductive dancer has been intermixed with the image of the repulsive vagabond. False images and stereotypes can be found in everyday language. They are reinforced in the media, in popular literature and children's books. *The Encyclopaedia Britannica* (in the now superseded 1956 edition) wrote: "The mental age of an average adult Gypsy is thought to be about that of a child of ten".

These stereotypes merely reflect and reinforce what is already widespread in public opinion. The same image is reinforced by photographs in local newspapers of roadside camps with piles of what seems to be rubbish but is, in fact, scrap waiting to be sold. But people fail to realise, or to admit, that this is because they are living on unhealthy, poorly located and inadequate sites. Gorgios also fail to realise that the Romanies have a high code of cleanliness, without which they would never have been able to survive in such unfit conditions.

Thus, not only does the image serve to rationalise the measures taken but the measures in turn reinforce the image. This vicious circle provides the basis for further violations of the Gypsies' human rights.

Women

The image of the enticing and sexually provocative Gypsy dancer, as illustrated by Merimée's nineteenth century story *Carmen* is still a feature of modern thought. Today's stereotype is usually romantic, a dark-haired beautiful girl, dressed in shabby but flowing fabrics, swinging her hips as she moves. Seduction is the key idea, the Great Temptress. Every few years, the 'Romany' motif hits the fashion pages. However, once aged, the Gypsy woman becomes an evil old crone with dangerous supernatural powers. Thus, either young or old, Gypsy women are never seen except as such stereotypes.

The romantic image of the young Gypsy woman is in total contrast to the derogatory stereotype of the Gypsy male. The reason for this is that a handsome Gypsy male would be a potential threat to the house-dwelling family, as illustrated in D. H. Lawrence's story *The Virgin and the Gypsy*. So, as a rule the Gypsy male is portrayed as a dirty thief and vagabond which lessens this threat. It is not, however, necessary to degrade the image of the Gypsy woman as, in our patriarchal society, women do not pose a threat; the Gorgio man is considered to have a much greater self-control and to be able to resist seduction.

When we examine the role which women play within the Gypsy community it becomes clear that the stereotype is incorrect. At home, Gypsy women must live up to a great many expectations. Rather than seduction, sex before marriage is condemned as is adultery even to the extent that a married woman should not be on her own with another man, especially a Gorgio man.

In the media

The popular and local press often run stories on Gypsies, usually with sensational headlines.

Armed police swoop on gypsies
Gypsies take over another car park
Council fights on against caravans
Fury at yes to travellers site
Gypsy camp barred in terror alert
New gypsy invasion alarm
Barriers go up to keep out gypsies
Gypsy camp threat to sheep farm
Fight over gypsy plan

The *Hornsey Journal* printed a picture of rubbish on an illegal site, accompanied by a leading article:

At a time when kiddies' playgrounds are being closed down and the cost of old people's meals is being increased, Haringey Council is spending

half a million pounds on building a permanent Travellers' site and a
further £400,000 on running its gay and lesbian committee.

Whether Romany or Irish, the papers don't like Travellers. In 1987 *The
Universe* interviewed a local parish priest under the heading:

Trained thieves cash in on underground passengers
Father K. said: 'I suspect most of these people are Travellers. They are
not very popular around here. They thieve and get drunk and smash
up pubs. The kids are uncontrollable. Some Travellers are squatting
in houses that are needed by homeless people.

Brochures issued by British Tour Operators reinforce the message:

Pickpockets
The most skilful thieves are groups of Gypsy children who roam the main
tourist areas of Paris and the Metro. Do not stop if approached by these
children and never take out your purse or wallet to give them anything as
it is likely to be snatched. (From Thomsons Guide Book).

In Mallorca as in all tourist locations all over the world we have a problem with thieves. Here, the Gypsies are the offenders. Don't buy any
jewellery or flowers or clothes from them. Gypsies in Mallorca are all
professional pickpockets. (From Airtours brochure).

The arrival of asylum seekers from eastern Europe also brought out
the headlines:

New immigrant crisis as gypsies invade Heathrow
Taxpayers taken for ride by gypsy gatecrashers
They couldn't find my dying granny a bed but they open the wards
for gypsies
Invasion of the giro czechs

The mediaeval accusation of stealing children still surfaces in the
popular press. In November 1998 the supposed sighting of a lost
English boy in a Greek village led the Sun to quote the grandfather –
not for the first time – as saying: "Gypsies are heavily involved in the
trade (of child abduction)". Many other papers then picked up the story,
including the broadsheet Scotsman.

Yet at the same time the Gypsies can be romantic, a phenomena of

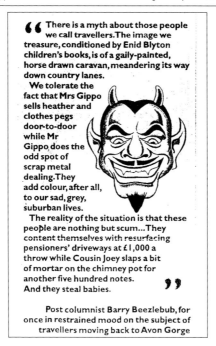

There is a myth about those people we call travellers. The image we treasure, conditioned by Enid Blyton children's books, is of a gaily-painted, horse drawn caravan, meandering its way down country lanes.

We tolerate the fact that Mrs Gippo sells heather and clothes pegs door-to-door while Mr Gippo does the odd spot of scrap metal dealing. They add colour, after all, to our sad, grey, suburban lives.

The reality of the situation is that these people are nothing but scum...They content themselves with resurfacing pensioners' driveways at £1,000 a throw while Cousin Joey slaps a bit of mortar on the chimney pot for another five hundred notes. And they steal babies.

Post columnist Barry Beezlebub, for once in restrained mood on the subject of travellers moving back to Avon Gorge

"And they steal babies...", the Beezelbub column in the *Bristol Evening Post* for the 28 March 1998. *Courtesy of the Bristol Evening Post and Prsss Ltd*

dual image that has persisted through the centuries. So, the *Daily Mirror* in July 1998:

> Josephine, a member of one of Britain's last true Romany families had dreamed of a fairy tale wedding. So her relatives organised an event fit for a princess. She was clad in a dazzling £10,000 white gown and she rode to church in a horse-drawn glass coach that cost £3,000 to hire. Her scrap dealing husband Patrick travelled in a princely carriage also pulled by horses.

But such stories do not always have a fairy tale ending. In June 1999 the Bristol County Court found that Cheltenham Borough Council had unlawfully discriminated against a Gypsy woman and her mother when it cancelled a booking for a wedding reception at Cheltenham's famed Pump Rooms. In the evidence before the court it was revealed that a borough official sent a memorandum on 9 July 1997 to local colleagues headed "Early warning system for new age travellers/gypsies" saying "this cross race" marriage may cause disputes and public order problems". The *Gloucestershire Echo* quoted from the memo just days later under the heading "Be ready for gipsy invasion" following up on the 16 July with a front page banner headline: "Big day axed in gipsy row: wedding guests are not our sort" (spelling and capitalisation as in original).

The Commission for Racial Equality has published a set of guidelines for the media and sent copies to the editors of every newspaper in the country (See Appendix 5)

In children's books

A false image of the Gypsy is imprinted in children from an early age. Heard in the school playground as a two ball game rhyme:

> Ipsy Gypsy wed in a tent
> She couldn't afford to pay the rent.
> So, when the rent man came next day
> Ipsy Gypsy ran away.

One book mentioning Gypsies found for the nursery age (3-5) in a recent survey was *Topsy and Tim's Friday Book* where Mother decides that her two children shall dress up as Gypsies for a fancy dress party. They put on something looking vaguely like a Spanish flamenco dancer's dress and win first prize. Children who had this book read to them in the school where it was found in the library would not connect the pictures with the Gypsy women in the campsite up the road from the school.

For the primary school, there are now some good non-fiction books. Many, however, generalise, such as *Gypsies and Nomads* which leaves the impression that all Gypsies have trained bears that dance to a tambourine. The traditional folk song *The Raggle Taggle Gypsy* reinforces the stereotype of a, for once, handsome Gypsy luring away the Gorgio lady (although the original Scottish ballad has a Gorgio lord luring away a Gypsy girl and then locking her up so she cannot go back to the camp).

> '…Tell me how could you leave your house and your land
> how could you leave your money-o
> how could you leave your only wedded lord
> all for the raggle taggle Gypsy-o
>
> Well, what care I for my house and my land
> what care I for my money-o
> tonight I lie in the wide open field
> in the arms of a raggle taggle, Gypsy-o.'

Standard works on history, geography and social studies for the second-ary school rarely mention Gypsies. A check on the indexes of ten such works in a London library (now an aquarium) for teachers produced the following figures.

References to	
Afro-Caribbeans or West Indians	10
Jews	6
Asians (including Indians and Pakistanis)	4
Gypsies or Romanies	0

The library had on its shelves *Tales and Legends of the Serbians* which describes Gypsies as cunning persons whose main occupation is stealing and selling horses, but none of the recent studies of Gypsies were in the education or sociology sections.

Children's comics still portray male Gypsies as spies, kidnappers or thieves while the Gypsy girl is often a frustrated ballet dancer whose parents will not let her go to school and who has to be smuggled into the classroom by well-wishing schoolgirls.

A privately published study of children's fiction by the Manchester teacher, Dennis Binns, shows how the myths are still current. Gypsies steal things:

> I lost it in town. I know it. This little Gypsy thief stole it from me.

and they steal children too:

> Very likely of noble birth and stolen by Gypsies and stained brown and now they are afraid of pursuit and have left it.

The standard classics read by older children and adults reinforce the stereotypes. Hugo's *Notre Dame de Paris* (filmed as *The Hunchback of Notre Dame*) has a girl stolen at birth by Gypsies, as does Cervantes' *La Gitanilla* (the Gypsy Girl). Heathcliffe in *Wuthering Heights* is another villain while in Lawrence's *The Virgin and the Gypsy* (also a film) we have the eternal seducer.

Prejudice in practice – opposition to caravan sites

We find ourselves today still with two stereotyped images of the Gypsy. The romantic image of the 'real Gypsy' who is living somewhere else or who died out in the Nineteenth century and the demonised image of the 'dirty Gypsy' who is the one in poverty asking for a caravan site in the neighbourhood. The first hint of a proposal for a council or private site brings out the petitions and the public meetings, the 'Residents Action Group' and the same arguments.

The expressed reasons for opposing a site are that Gypsies don't pay rates and taxes and leave a mess. House values will go down (the same argument is used against a hostel for ex-psychiatric patients) or the school will be overcrowded (the same argument is used against a new council estate). Sometimes the Gypsies' own welfare is invoked. The proposed site is too near a main road and the children would get run over. The Gypsies would be unhappy in a middle class area.

One reason may be envy. The Gypsies round a camp fire on the illegal site in the corner of the park don't seem to work from nine to five, women and children bob in and out of each other's caravans in a way unknown to those watching from the windows of the high-rise flats nearby and, if they want, they can hitch up their caravans and go to the other end of the country without asking anyone.

Here are a selection of the arguments that have been made against sites either in the press or in letters sent to councils and planning inspectors. First, opposing sites proposed by local councils under the 1968 Caravan Sites Act:

> If the proposal goes through I will be forced to give up farming because of the problems that would arise from stray dogs from the camp. (Kent)

> The close proximity of these people of possibly Irish origin to the Royal Armament Establishment is a real risk. (Kent)

The presence of Travellers means higher insurance rates for us, difficulties in attracting clients to our business, difficulties in attracting employees and rubbish everywhere. (Hackney)

I myself would be extremely concerned about the welfare of the children in my care and would not like to guarantee their safety at all times. (Teacher in Essex)

The following are extracts from letters opposing a private site for one family in a village in Bedfordshire:

My property has become virtually unsaleable at a stroke and in the future might at best eventually become saleable but at considerably reduced value.

This land is directly opposite the village play area. I am only one of the many parents, with a two year old son, who would not be able to allow my child to visit this play area for fear of what may happen to them.

This site is opposite the children's recreation area. It is felt that Gypsies often have a variety of vehicles and sometimes fierce dogs which would be a possible hazard to the children.

Crime within the village has already started to escalate, I am told. Should this rise even further, who will fund the police patrols that will be required to restore some sort of normality to the village?

Move them on and let us respectable council-tax paying law abiding citizens of H. village remain that way. These Gypsies cost us hundreds or even thousands of pounds. This money should be spent on the health services etc.

The site is very close to the Royal Oak pub and we feel this represents a potential problem in terms of public order.

These bungalows are homes for pensioners and we live a very peaceful life here and the last thing we need at our time of life is trouble and filth with Gypsies.

In this last case, a petition with 608 names opposing the site was sent to the council.

When a properly run local authority or private site does open, the previous fears are usually seen to be unjustified.

Even a proposal for a museum by the Romany Guild encountered vitriolic opposition. Again these are extracts from letters to the local council:

> I object to this proposal as Gypsies are filthy, they bring filth and they leave filth. They are thieves and they pay for nothing. I pay rates, I pay tax and my house is clean. The price of my house would be devalued and I would physically participate in removing them. We don't want them here ever.

> A Gypsy museum would … encourage the visitation in large and regular quantities of Gypsies, Travellers, itinerants and other unsavoury characters from all over the country. Waltham Abbey will deteriorate into a slum area.

The proposal for the museum was rejected by an Inspector from the Department of the Environment as 'unsuitable for the area', even though there is an educational farm centre and a proposed glasshouse museum within a couple of miles. A later application for a museum in a more isolated part of Essex has also been turned down. Meanwhile, Gypsy museums have been opened in northern Greece and even in Tarnow in Poland and Brno in the Czech Republic.

Prejudice often turns to violence against an illegal site that seems to be becoming permanent, or 'tolerated' to use the terminology of government circulars. In 1968 Gypsies came to Greenland Road in Sheffield. Fifty local residents attacked the camp. The Gypsies moved twice, ending up in Tinsley Park. Local residents produced a petition accusing the Gypsies of 'nude bathing in the boating lake and allowing horses to mate in public'. In July of that year a mob of 200 marched on the caravans and had to be persuaded to return home by the newly elected Conservative councillor for the area.

In Kent, a youth club leader led a gang which threw a fire-bomb at caravans. He was later caught and sent to prison. Shots were fired at another caravan in Kent so regularly that the owner bought a tall van which he placed between his home and the road to protect it. Near Bedford in 1970 a paving stone was thrown through the window of a caravan, narrowly missing a young girl in bed.

These incidents have continued sporadically. In 1994 there were several attacks on Gypsy caravans returning south from Appleby Fair. A group of caravans camping on derelict land in Watlington near Oxford were attacked by vigilantes. Four caravans and nine cars were smashed up. An axe was thrown at a grandmother. A police camera managed to film nineteen of the attackers of whom fifteen were identified. However, nobody was prosecuted. A police spokesman said that an old man had been held up and robbed at about the same time as the attack on the camp. It was a more serious case and the vigilante attack 'had to sit on the back burner'.

Incitement to racial hatred

Sections of the 1976 Race Relations Act and the Public Order Act of 1936 cover incitement to racial hatred. There have been few prosecutions since 1939 under the Public Order Act and none in cases concerning Gypsies.

Sections of the Public Order Act of 1986 update the Public Order Act of 1936, an Act originally designed to cover anti-Semitic propaganda. During the debate in the House of Lords in October 1986 Lord Elwyn-Jones twice tried to get an amendment into the Bill to clarify that 'Gypsies are a group of persons defined by reference to race'. He cited the CRE which had told him that about a third of the complaints it receives are about hate literature relating to Gypsies.

> They are among the most abused and insulted people in this country. Indeed the language is cruder and more offensive than literature relating to Blacks or Jews which has been or is being prosecuted.

The Earl of Caithness, while rejecting the amendment, affirmed:

> We are concerned to see that written material which stirs up racial hatred against Gypsies who are of a distinct ethnic group should be penalised in the same way as any other ethnic or racial group ... When there is evidence that activity of the kinds penalised by Part III (of the Act) has been directed against them, my right honourable friend the Attorney General has authorised me to say that he will consider instituting proceedings in exactly the same way as he would in respect of any other ethnic group.

> An individual Gypsy cannot take action under this Act. The case has to be reported to the police and then the Attorney General can prosecute. Heartened by the debate in the House of Lords, Eli Frankham of the National Romany Rights Group tried once again to get action over a leaflet which had been circulated in Norfolk:

Gypsies at Tilney for ever

Without consultation, Norfolk County Council is proposing a permanent Gypsy site at Tilney. It may not be at the bottom of your garden but it will affect you as if it were.

Your property will be devalued as much as 50 per cent

Will you be happy about leaving your property unattended?

Will your school remain at the same high standard?

The dogs – the rubbish – the smell – the scrap – the rodents

Remember if we don't harass the Council now we shall be harassed for the rest of our lives.

In 1985 the Solicitor General had written that he was not satisfied that the leaflet infringed the 1936 Act and that he did not propose to do anything about it. Following the House of Lords debate, Mr Frankham wrote again. This time it was the Attorney General's Chambers who replied:

> The assurance given by the Attorney General in the Committee Stage of the (1986) Public Order Bill does not I regret alter the decision made in the matter to which you refer. It has always been the case that there may be circumstances where Gypsies may be considered an ethnic group for the purposes of section 5A of the Public Order Act 1936. However, in order to establish that the 'Gypsies' referred to were an ethnic group, it must be shown that the reference was to true Romany Gypsies, rather than Travellers, tinkers, etc.

So, to sum up the working of the 1986 Public Order Act: the 'trespass' clause was not intended to apply to Gypsies, but was being used against them daily, while the 'incitement to racial hatred' provisions were intended to help Gypsies but in practice they will not.

In 1970 the Conurbation Action Groups in the Midlands distributed leaflets during the local elections which read:

> Consider the facts before you give your (X)

> Tinkers
> Extensive areas invaded by Irish Tinkers. Elderly citizens and communi-

> ties terrorised. Industry and commerce subjected to the highest crime
> wave on record. Provide Tinker sites and in doing so solve the Republic
> of Ireland's Tinker problem.

The leaflet went on to deal with the danger of mixing white and black
races which indicates clearly their racist position on such matters.

In 1986 Leeds City Council advertised the following post:

> Assistant Gypsy Liaison Officer/Clinic Attendant to assist in the enforce-
> ment of the Council's policies on Gypsies. Additionally the person will
> assist in the Clinic in the treatment of male clients, frequently vagrants,
> for lice, fleas, scabies and similar conditions.

Complaints were made about the tone of this advertisement by
Gypsy civil rights groups and individuals. The CRE began an action
against the City Council but did not pursue it. Although unpleasant it
was not incitement to racial hatred. Leeds Council remained unmoved
by the protests and no apology was forthcoming. Mr Rawnsley, Chief
Officer, replied to a letter of complaint:

> The Council did reissue the advertisement in question to make it perfect-
> ly plain that the two functions of the post advertised i.e. Assistant Gypsy
> Liaison Officer and Assistant Attendant at the Disinfestation Clinic were
> entirely separate and simply a question of working practice.

The leading anti-fascist magazine *Searchlight* has reported harassment by
fascists of a Gypsy boxer and a later article highlighted a racist leaflet
disseminated in Oldham, while a National Front march in Lewisham
included on its route the local Gypsy site. Gypsies defending the site
were arrested and charged with assault. The recent arrival of Romany
asylum seekers in Dover has led to at least two big marches organised by
the National Front during which anti-racist protesters were arrested
while no action has been taken against the racist leaflets distributed by
the National Front. With the publication of the Stephen Lawrence
Inquiry Report in February 1999, attention has once again turned to the
situation of 'race relations' in Britain and what the future may hold. It is
too soon to tell if the McPherson Report will have a lasting impact, but
it is hoped that any new legislation which arises from the Report will
also include and protect Gypsies and other Travellers from racial discrimination and racist violence.

5

The struggle for caravan sites

The disappearing *hatchin tan* (stopping place)

We noted earlier that there was a short period after 1945 where Gypsies led a comparatively untroubled life in harmony with the house-dwelling community for whom they provided useful services. Two factors were to change this. First, the movement of their 'customers' from the country to towns, which had started with industrialisation as early as 1850, gathered speed after the Second World War. This meant that Gypsies, too, had to move into towns in order to earn their living but in the towns they found it harder to find stopping places and also came into contact with local police and council officials who were not used to seeing a Gypsy caravan amongst the willowherb on their old bomb site. They had not met Gypsies before and had no sympathy for their life-style.

The second factor was the conflict over land use, especially in the south-east. Empty plots in otherwise built-up areas were bought up and built on, disused aerodromes – popular stopping places since 1945 because of the concrete runways – were taken over for new housing or industrial estates, and motorways with no grass verges replaced roads. The prefabricated houses and mobile homes which many Gypsies had bought and used as a home base after 1945 became dilapidated and an eyesore to local councillors who wanted them replaced by the newly popular high-rise flats.

Moving on

As their traditional stopping places disappeared Gypsies were moved on by mobile police and council workmen more often and in a more brutal way than by the local country policemen.

The reality of moving on is described here in one of many accounts reported by the Safe Childbirth Foundation:

> We were stopping on a piece of waste ground in Islington. I was working. It was 7.0 am. I had just arrived at my workplace when the phone rang. It was my daughter M. Mum come home quick, the bulldozers are here. The council workers cleared a path through the rubble and towed the trailers out into the street with landrovers. We threw gas bottles, churns and anything else we could rescue into the moving caravans. The caravans and their contents were taken and locked up in hall. We set out in the rain with our dogs to follow on foot. The caretaker of the hall told me he was locking up. I asked if I could come back later to collect some dry clothes. He said I would have to come back the next day. As M. looked all in and was pregnant with her first child I sent her off to the housing office to find a place in a hostel for the night.
>
> When I got to the hall the next morning the caretaker said I could have five minutes to get everything I wanted. It was another day before I could get the caravan out and find a new site. As we drew up, a council officer arrived with a notice to shift. We had two days to get off!

At an eviction in Edmonton, north-east London, in May 1998 police and town hall officials ordered Travellers, including a twelve year old boy, to drive their caravans off an open space. In the process, six year-old Patrick Dooley was run over and killed.

Gypsies may be pulled off with or without a court order, or taken to court and fined. Travelling families stopping on the roadside could be and were prosecuted under a statute dating from 1822. This made it an offence to 'be a Gypsy encamping on the highway', and was still used until it was finally repealed in 1980. Under this legislation Gypsies on the roadside verge or in a lay-by were committing an offence while, in theory, a foreign tourist or British holidaymaker would be able to park a caravan next to them without being summonsed. Now all caravans are subject to the same legislation, the 1994 Criminal Justice Act.

Many local authorities have Local Acts of Parliament, dating from the 1930s, which give them additional powers. Thus, the Surrey Act of 1931 enables district councils to draw a circle of 880 yards radius around any one caravan and ban any 'movable dwelling' from stopping within that circle for ever. A Mr Giles was fined at Guildford in 1969 under this Act, for having a chalet (adjudged by the court to be a movable dwelling) on land which he owned.

A determined police force can soon drive a family out of their patch. A Gypsy was imprisoned overnight in Havering Borough for the offence of 'driving a vehicle [his lorry and caravan] across the pavement' which he had done in order to reach a few feet of anonymous grass to stop for the night, after being evicted in the morning. The next day he was fined £30 and not surprisingly moved to the next county. This family has never been able to get on a site and the children had only a few days of education from time to time. Early in 1994 the now grown-up son of this same Gypsy was fined £500 for stopping on his own land without planning permission and in 1998 again was refused planning permission by an Inspector following a public enquiry to place his caravan on land owned by his father. Another generation of children are deprived of schooling while he searches for a permanent winter base.

If all else fails a request to 'show me a receipt for every item in the caravan down to the teaspoons' or be arrested and taken to court for receiving stolen property will usually have the desired effect. Local authorities have become more ingenious in barring off empty pieces of land – ditches, low barriers on car parks, wooden and metal posts, banks of earth (often hastily planted with rose bushes) are used to prevent caravans driving on to any open land. Unions representing local authority workers have told their members not to evict Gypsies but councils now employ private firms of security guards to do this work. With or without court orders, the majority of the nearly 3,000 families still unable to get on to a site are moved on after a few days or weeks and have to look for a new place to stop.

As Carmel told listeners to the BBC's *Woman's Hour* in August 1998:

> The police came and said if we weren't gone by the Monday morning they were going to come with armed officers with firearms to move us all. The children couldn't believe it; they looked at each other really frightened and so I said.' Let's get off here, we're not going to stay if they're going to come, we imagined something off the telly, like in Ireland or something. It's just unbelievable what they'll do to you so we just moved.
>
> You'd never be able to take the children to a play group or anything like that round here because you just don't get the time to do it, and

somedays they're stuck in a lorry perhaps eight hours at a time. For instance a little while ago in Southend we had helicopters above us. I think there were ten squad cars and we said. 'Are we murderers?' They were blocking every junction on the motorway and wouldn't let us off and I said for instance, if my child needed to go to the hospital, I couldn't get off that motorway to get the turning for the hospital.' The policeman said. 'That's not my problem, that's yours.'

We look below at attempts by the government to encourage local councils to provide stopping places.

The Caravan Sites Act of 1960

In 1960 the Government introduced legislation to control private caravan sites – The Caravan Sites (Control of Development) Act. The new law made it difficult for Gypsies to buy small plots of land and winter on them. Section l of the Act spelt this out clearly:

> No occupier of land shall after the commencement of this Act cause or permit any part of the land to be used (as a caravan site) unless he is the holder of a site licence.

You cannot get a site licence unless you have planning permission. After 1960 anyone buying a piece of land had to get first planning permission and then a site licence before they could put a caravan on it. Exceptions were made for 'established sites' and a number of cases were heard over the following years asking for the recognition that the land had 'established use' as a caravan site. It was not always easy to prove that the site had been in use before 1960. The H. family lost the right to remain on their land near Heathrow Airport because the word of the retired Enforcement Officer as to which side of a hedge caravans had been parked fourteen years earlier was believed rather than the statements of the families themselves. They had been refused planning permission because of the danger of 'low flying aircraft' even though houses had been built in the neighbouring village, not to mention luxury hotels on the edge of the airport. Many years later, the Council realised that it would be cheaper and less trouble to abandon the search for an alternative site and let the families stay where they were.

The existence of a caravan site before 1960 and the obtaining of an

Established Use Certificate was still no guarantee that the families would be left alone. Local councils were to take over the sites by compulsory purchase and either keep the Gypsies on as their tenants, as in the case of Harrow Manorway (now called Thistlebrook) in Greenwich and Outwood (Surrey), or evict them and build houses as was to happen in Greenways, also in Surrey.

In addition, other Gypsies were driven on to the roadside as private landowners who previously let them stop on their land would no longer do so as they had to get a site licence. The 1960 Caravan Sites Act was also used against farmers who let Gypsies stay on their land before or after the days when they were actually working on the crops.

In and out of Parliament

For many years neither the Lords nor the Commons had discussed the Gypsies but this was to change with the election in 1945 of Norman Dodds as Labour MP for Dartford, which contained several shanty towns on the Thames Marshes. Until his death, twenty years later, he was to campaign in the House of Commons on behalf of their inhabitants.

He helped to set up a Committee with Gypsy and Gorgio members which in 1947 drew up a nine-point *Charter*. Its demands included:

- a survey to be taken of the number of Romanies and other Travellers in England and Wales.
- adequate provision of camps with water, sanitation, ablutions, and communal centre facilities.
- a suitable scheme for the educating of Gypsy children.
- consideration given to the practicability of training young Romanies as teachers for the education of Romany children in established camps.

In 1950 Dodds was much moved by an old Gypsy woman from Manchester who had travelled to ask his help. Her husband had been called up to the army and killed in Italy during World War II. She and her daughter had been evicted from the piece of land that they owned and had lived on for over twenty years until a Compulsory Purchase Order had displaced them. For the past two years they had been hounded from place to place. In November of the same year he was to ask the first question on this subject for many years:

> Mr Dodds asked the Minister of Health what steps he was taking to alleviate the serious position that is developing for Gypsies in finding places where they and their caravans can be accommodated.

> Mr Bevan (Labour Minister of Health). 'I am considering with my Right Honourable Friend the Home Secretary what information is available to us on this matter and am not yet in a position to say what further steps may be required.

It was to be fifteen years before the Government had sufficient information available to them. However, in 1951 Norman Dodds initiated a debate in the Commons and on 9 May Hugh Dalton received a deputation of Gypsies. Then there followed a General Election. Norman Dodds, now an opposition MP, had to turn his attention to the new Conservative Housing Minister, Harold Macmillan. Macmillan agreed to a pilot survey in Kent which Dodds later felt was a delaying tactic to keep him quiet.

Meanwhile, Dartford Rural District Council evicted 200 men, women and children from Drench Wood. *The Times* was moved to write in a leader of 'the victims whose helplessness merits sympathy'. Following the publicity aroused by the eviction of these families, Dr Charles Hill, by then Minister of Housing, agreed to make a national survey of Gypsies.

But, things were happening. Norman Dodds himself opened, not without opposition, a private site. The novelist Barbara Cartland built another in Hertfordshire, while the then Strood Council (in Kent) opened one of the earliest local authority sites. Dodds died suddenly in 1965, three years before the passing of a new Caravan Sites Act, which owed much to his endeavours. By then others had joined the struggle.

The Caravan Sites Act of 1968

We referred above to the survey initiated by Charles Hill in 1962. Replies from local councils were voluntary and sparse. In 1964 a new Government took office and a new Minister of Housing, Richard Crossman, decided to get things moving. On 22 March 1965 a national survey of Gypsies took place. It recorded some 15,500 'Gypsies and other Travellers', perhaps 75 per cent of the real number, but a start had been made and the Government and its civil servants could no longer claim, as had Aneurin Bevan in 1950, that there was not enough information available.

The report of this survey was published in 1967 under the title Gypsies and Other Travellers. It found that 60 per cent of the families had travelled in the previous year. In many cases this travelling was not voluntary but the result of harassment by the police and council officials. Few children received any regular schooling. Only 33 per cent of the families had access to a water supply. There were few local authority sites, even though the 1960 Caravan Sites Act had given councils the power to set up caravan sites.

In this same year the Government offered to support Eric Lubbock (later Lord Avebury) with his private bill dealing with the scandalous practices of some private mobile home owners in return for his adding a second part on the subject of Gypsy sites. It is still a matter of debate as to whether these provisions were introduced because of, or in spite of, the campaigning of the newly formed Gypsy Council. Thomas Acton (in *Gypsy Politics and Social Change*) analyses this debate and we shall not attempt to improve on his analysis.

The major provisions of the 1968 Caravan Sites Act, as it affected Gypsies, were:

- County Councils and London Boroughs had a duty to provide accommodation for Gypsies residing in and resorting to their areas.
- A London Borough did not need to provide accommodation for more than fifteen caravans. (Section 6)
- The Secretary of State for the Environment could give directions to any local authority requiring them to provide sites. These directions were enforceable by *mandamus*. (Section 9)
- An area could be designated as an area in which Gypsies may not station their caravans except if there are pitches free on an official site. It was a criminal offence to do so. (Sections 10 and 11).

Gypsies were defined in the Act as 'persons of nomadic habit of life, whatever their race or origin'. This definition has now been moved restrospectively to the 1960 Act.

The provisions of Section 11 of the 1968 Act enabled a constable to arrest without warrant anyone who organised the sort of passive resistance to evictions which the Gypsy Council had encouraged during 1967, while the designation provisions of Section 10 were compared, with some degree of accuracy, by Gypsy spokespersons as similar to the Pass Laws and apartheid once operating in South Africa. In the following section, we look at the working of the 1968 Act. The Gypsy Council argued for the immediate setting up of a chain of temporary but official sites and in areas where the Council was strong such sites were opened, often with primitive facilities but at least providing a haven from police and bailiffs.

The 1968 Caravan Sites Act, in so far as it affected Gypsies, came into force on 1 April 1970. Some may consider this a well chosen date as the Gypsies were certainly fooled into thinking there was to be some rapid improvement in their living conditions. After a two-year wait for this part of the Act to come into force, the late George Marriott and other activists in Bedfordshire organised a celebration of 'Gypsy Independence Day'. Gypsies and supporters came from London and elsewhere, a bonfire was lit, songs were sung and everyone thought that the long years of harassment had ended. In fact, it was to be a hard struggle for Gypsies, their supporters, sympathetic councillors and officials before a realistic number of sites were provided. The tables in the first chapter show what progress had been made by the time we went to press and that several thousand families are still waiting for a site. Children born in 1970 are now twenty-nine and many of them have, in spite of circulars from the Government urging an end to harassment and the provision of temporary sites, spent these years on the move and unable to get regular schooling.

In particular, district councils often held up the attempts of county councils to open sites. Worse still, the 1960 Caravan Sites Act was used by district councils to get Gypsies off land in their area owned by the county council, even when the county council was following the government recommendations not to harass families. So, in 1972 the now defunct Caterham and Warlingham Urban District Council used the 1960 Act to take Surrey County Council to court for 'permitting land to be used as a caravan site without a licence', that is to say, not evicting some Gypsies parked in a field in Tupwood Lane. The case was heard at

Myma Butler (second left at top) was born in this traditional bender tent but is bringing up her own family in a caravan on a council site in Hertfordshire (on left holding her first grandchild) just a few miles from where she was born; *photographs by Tim Devlin and Bill Forster*

Caterham on 26 June, the barrister representing the Gypsies was not allowed to address the court as it was ruled that the Gypsies 'had no interest in the matter' and the County Council was found guilty and fined £40. After a similar case in Hertfordshire, the Government stepped in and now a county council does not need a licence to run a site. The Department of the Environment, Transport and the Regions can, however, call in a controversial site proposal for a public enquiry. Only for a short period around 1977 while the late Donald Byrne was Gypsy Sites Officer at the Ministry of Housing (forerunner of the Department of the Environment) did central government exert any pressure on councils to set up sites.

The Cripps Report

In 1977 the Government, aware of the shortcomings of the 1968 Act, or rather the way in which local authorities had ignored its provisions, commissioned John Cripps to make a rapid one-person study of the workings of the Act. Although he was not asked to make a detailed study like that which produced the 1965 Report (*Gypsies and Other Travellers*) he did, nevertheless, write an impressive document.

Following this, the Labour Government introduced a new Caravan Sites Bill, embodying many of his suggestions. Unfortunately for the Gypsies this Labour Government was to fall before all stages of the Bill could get through Parliament. Some of Cripps' suggestions were later to be incorporated in the 1980 Local Government Act.

Designation – Gypsy-free zones

Under the 1968 Act, 'designated' areas of the country were those where Gypsies could not station a caravan on vacant pieces of land without committing a crime. In 1972 the first designations were proposed – the then County Boroughs of Plymouth, St Helens and Stoke, followed in the same year by Manchester, Richmond on Thames and Wolverhampton. Plymouth kept its status and the powers that went with it even though it had not had a site for many years. Legally it was still a Gypsy-free zone. Apart from a short pause while John Cripps (see above) was reviewing the working of the Act, the process of designation continued right up to 1994, encompassing whole counties such as Dorset and West Sussex.

What did designation mean in practice? It should have meant that all the Gypsies usually resident in an area had been provided with pitches and that there were some pitches in reserve for families 'resorting to' the area for short periods, whether for work or to visit relatives. All Gypsies would have to stop on a site. This would not have been unreasonable if pitches had been available. In practice it meant providing the minimum number of pitches that the district could get away with, based on an inadequate census that missed perhaps 10 per cent of families on the roadside and 50 per cent of those on private sites, and then denying access to the area for any caravans that arrived in transit.

In 1986 West Sussex (designated in 1982) claimed, in terms more appropriate to a Balkan war than to a programme of social aid, "to be on the verge of victory in its battle to sweep away unauthorised Gypsy caravan sites from the county's roadsides", as the *West Sussex Gazette* put it.

Since the county had a duty to provide for any Gypsy families 'residing in or resorting to' the area, we may wonder why there should be any caravans on the roadside at all. At any rate we would have hoped that the Council was *sweeping* these families from the roadside on to officially provided sites. However, in the year prior to this statement, forty-three caravans had come into the county. They were served with summonses immediately and warned that, if they did not move voluntarily out of the county, court action would be taken.

The Government's decision to designate was apparently infallible. In reply to a letter pointing out that there were still unsited families in the four designated districts of Buckinghamshire, the County Secretary replied:

> Designation would not have been granted for the four districts if the Secretary of State had not at the time been satisfied that the proper provision had been made.

Yet there were thirty-three unsited caravans in July 1982 while designation was being considered and a count in March 1983 showed forty on the roadside proper and twelve more squatting on the edge of a full site.

The Government had the power to de-designate an area but this was never used. Under the proposals in the new Criminal Justice and

Public Order Act the powers previously available in designated areas have been strengthened and will apply across the whole of England (and Wales). They are available against all caravans, probably to stop New Travellers from defending any court proceedings by claiming they are not Gypsies.

Life on a council site

During the debate on the 1968 Act, it was stressed that the intention was to provide 'a network of sites on which the Gypsies could continue their traditional way of life'. In January 1999 there were 329 council-run sites operating, providing some 5,216 pitches (34 pitches less than in January 1997). To what extent has the intention of the Act been carried out?

In the first place there are not enough sites or pitches. This in itself brings many problems. Families are afraid to leave a site in order to seek work in case they cannot get a pitch when they want to return. They may then have to move to another site and find a new school for their children and a new doctor. More likely they will end up on the roadside, or – unwanted – in a car park or a sports field. A few enlightened authorities do allow Gypsies to reserve a pitch on payment of half or full rent for a limited number of weeks each summer.

The least provided for are the 'long-distance' Travellers with their specialised trades such as gate-making and tarmac'ing drives, who need to travel all the year round. In the past they often stopped on private land and paid rent but the working of the 1960 Act has ended this. Transit sites or transit pitches on residential sites have been suggested in Government circulars but there is little such provision. The Government set up an enquiry (for which they imported two sociologists from America) and this recommended a chain of Government-run sites along the major motorways. The report (*The Special Accommodation needs of long-distance and regional Travellers*) has been ignored.

The social life of Gypsies has been changed by the way official sites are organised. The most popular number for pitches is sixteen, comprising fifteen caravans and a warden's hut, all neatly marked out with white paint to the same size and numbered. The figure of fifteen is based on the minimum number for which London Boroughs had to provide. In

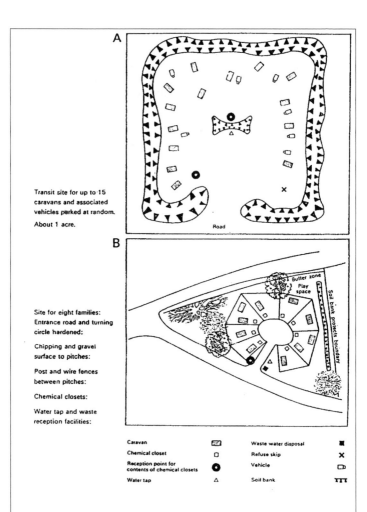

A

Transit site for up to 15 caravans and associated vehicles parked at random.
About 1 acre.

Road

B

Site for eight families:
Entrance road and turning circle hardened:

Chipping and gravel surface to pitches:

Post and wire fences between pitches:

Chemical closets:

Water tap and waste reception facilities:

Buffer zone

Play space

Soil bank protects boundary

Caravan		Waste water disposal	
Chemical closet		Refuse skip	✗
Reception point for contents of chemical closets	●	Vehicle	
Water tap	△	Soil bank	

From DoE Circular No. 28/77

PLAN A
Transit site for up to fifteen caravans and associated vehicles parked at random. About one acre.

PLAN B
Site for eight families: entrance road and turning circle hardened, chipping and gravel surface to pitches, post and wire fences between pitches, chemical closets, water tap and wate reception facilities.

the past, Gypsies could choose their own neighbours when they stopped in a field. Now the Council decides who will occupy any vacant pitch on the basis of a points system similar to that used for housing vacancies. Two families from groups which have traditionally been at loggerheads may find themselves unwilling neighbours. If in-laws come to visit there are further problems. In the past they would pull up their caravan alongside and while keeping their own cooking and sleeping facilities would be able to enjoy the company of children and grandchildren for a few days. Nowadays they have to leave their own caravan behind and sleep in a perhaps already overcrowded caravan. The same applies to a mother who wants to come and help her daughter before or after the birth of a new baby or an aged parent that a family would like to have nearby. Caravans arriving to attend a funeral or wedding add to the problems. The old freedom has gone.

No allowance is made either for children growing up. As they get older the family needs two caravans so that sons and daughters can sleep apart. Many councils then insist on a one caravan per pitch rule and so the family has to rent a second pitch – if they can afford it. This pitch may well not be adjacent to the parents' caravan. There has been some friction on sites where one family has tried to create vacancies for other relatives to move on.

Bureaucratic procedures make it difficult to get on a site. These regulations from Nuneaton are typical. An applicant for a pitch has to fill in a two-page form. In addition to what seem to be reasonable requests for information such as details of the caravan, the form asks for more:

> How many vehicles do you have at the present time?
> Have you any regular occupation? (give details)
> Name of employer
> Have you occupied any other local authority site?
> If so where?

After completing the form the applicant apparently has to return to the roadside but keep in touch to find out whether they have been accepted for a pitch. Once on the site they have to abide by the seventeen conditions of this licence including the following:

> The caravan must be of proprietary manufacture and of an external colour approved by the Council.

Not all council sites bar animals.
A beautifully groomed horse and 'silkie' (exercise cart) in front of a 'mobile home' on a council site; *photograph by Bill Forster*

In addition to the seventeen conditions of the licence there are eleven 'site regulations' such as:

> No bonfires shall be lit on the site.
> No trade or business shall be carried out on any part of the site other than on vehicles [lorries] on individual plots.

Animals are restricted:

> The licensees shall not keep on the site any animals or poultry with the exception of a single domestic pet for which prior approval is obtained in writing from the Chief Housing Officer.

The Harrogate site bans animals completely:

> The Licensee shall not keep and shall not permit or suffer any person living with him to keep on the site any dogs poultry or any other animals.

Any Gypsies who are able and willing to accept these conditions, which mean radically changing their lifestyle, have to pay a deposit of £75 and four weeks rent in advance before being allowed on to the site. Tenants are allowed to vacate the site for a maximum of four weeks only to do seasonal work – much less than the normal summer agricultural season. While away they have to pay full rent and the Council informs the social security office that the family is away.

On the Harrogate site overnight guests are restricted:

> Only the persons named on the application form shall be resident in the caravan. No visitors will be allowed to stay on the site unless specific approval is received in advance to any exception.

Even if the families keep these conditions, they have no security. Caravan sites for Gypsies are specifically excluded from the protection of Part 1 of the 1968 Caravan Sites Act and the Mobile Homes Act. A Council can terminate the licence by giving notice at any time and the caravan family have to leave. The tenants of a Gypsy site have little recourse to the courts, a point confirmed in a recent judgement by the House of Lords in the case of Greenwich versus Powell. It was also ruled that the fact that Mr Powell himself no longer travelled and had lost his Gypsy status did not affect the status of the site. It was built as a Gypsy site and, therefore, the Council had the power to evict any tenant without a reason be they Gypsies or not. The irony of this particular case is that the Greenwich site had originally been privately owned by the Gypsies themselves.

In Bedfordshire, a Gypsy single parent was given notice because her brother and his wife had come and parked on her pitch over Christmas without her obtaining permission from the site warden – who was on leave at the time. In the same county, Mid-Bedfordshire District Council served notice to quit on Kath L. because the boyfriend of one of her daughters – who does not live on the site – was arrested on the site by the police for an alleged offence committed elsewhere. Kath is taking her case to the European Court of Human Rights.

These sites are not cheap. The Potton site in Bedfordshire charged £76 a week for the pitch and a wash-room. The families provide their own caravans. As a result of high rents, many of the licencees (Gypsies do not have security of tenure in law) on council sites have been forced on to social security to get housing benefit, as they cannot earn enough to pay these high sums. This situation is as true in Scotland and Wales as it is in England.

A new book (*Static Life on the Site*) gives a summary of the position on the Wakefield site, which as we have seen is equally applicable elsewhere:

> The [residents] are stuck on a site which apart from being in physically poor shape, lacking facilities and resources, and being poorly managed, does not allow them the control or autonomy necessary to live within their own traditions or extended family networks.

From January 1996 the rules governing the payment of Housing Benefit to tenants, whether living in houses or in a caravan on a council site, were changed. From that date all new tenants would only be able to claim a 'fair rent' as housing benefit and this would be based on a Local Reference Rent (LRR) determined by the Rent Officer. The tenant has to make up the shortfall between the fair rent and the rent that the landlord wants to charge.

In Mid Bedfordshire District Council a licencee who was formerly paying £70 a week for a pitch on the Potton caravan site moved back onto the same council site in January 1999 and had her LRR assessed at £27. Since she could not afford to pay the difference the District Council, which had an obligation to house her, decided to reduce the rent for all its licencees on council sites to the fair rent. Predictably, this decision was greeted with outrage by tenants of council houses whose views were reported in *Bedfordshire on Sunday* on the 6 June as follows:

> Gypsies' rents down – others pick up tab
> Council rents have been slashed by two thirds – but only for Gypsy tenants. One council tenant said "I might as well go and live in a bloody caravan. Our rents go up every year. Now my money is subsidising housing for Gypsies".

All tenants are subject to the new rules governing housing benefit and the fair rent assessment took account of the fact that the Gypsy licencee only received a concrete pitch and a brick built bathroom/kitchen.

The "mopping up" brigade on an unofficial site in the London area; *photograph by Phillip Wolmuth*

Transit sites

The 1968 Act spoke of provision for Gypsies 'residing in and resorting to an area'. It was assumed that provision for those resorting to an area would mean transit sites or transit pitches so that nomadic families could move around the country in search of work and find a pitch wherever they were. In practice, few local authorities have provided transit pitches while the proposed new planning policy for Malden (in Essex) states categorically that no transit sites will be permitted. Often transit pitches have been converted into permanent pitches to meet the demand for long-term stays.

The Courts and the Ombudsmen

Under the 1968 Caravan Sites Act the Secretary of State could order any local authority to provide additional sites but he had not used these powers when two Gypsies (Lee and Bond) requested him on their behalf to issue a Direction to Hertfordshire County Council to provide more sites. He refused to do so. In 1992 an application was made for judicial review of his decision and also for a declaration that Hertfordshire County Council was in breach of its statutory duty to provide sites. Although the Declaration against the County Council was made the Court refused, however, to make an order of *mandamus* against the Secretary of State that he should direct the County Council to provide the sites. As a result of this case, however, the Secretary of State did issue such a Direction but without a time limit and as a result the sites were not built. Subsequently, similar Directions were issued to Surrey County Council and Hereford and Worcester County Council that they were also in breach of their duty to provide sufficient sites.

Attempts were made to involve the Parliamentary Ombudsman (Commissioner for Administration) who is responsible for investigating complaints referred to him by members of the House of Commons where members of the public claim to have suffered injustice by reason of action taken by Government Departments. A member of the public complained that the Minister responsible had not used his powers to direct Avon to build sites and therefore the complainant was suffering from unauthorised caravans in a neighbouring road. The Commissioner ruled that insufficient time had elapsed since the County of Avon had been formed for them to have been able to form a policy and develop sites. Avon was later directed by the Secretary of State to provide more pitches.

Complaints to the other Ombudsman, the Local Government Commissioner responsible for complaints against the actions of local councils, were more successful:

- Hackney and Tower Hamlets were found guilty of maladministration in not providing a caravan site. Both councils have now done so.
- In 1984 Staffordshire County Council was criticised by the Ombudsman for 'taking ten years to get nowhere' in the provision of a site in the Lyme valley. No compensation was ever awarded to Gypsies for the lack of a site while the 1968 Caravan Sites Act was in force but Giorgio house-dwellers have been luckier.
- In 1988 the Commissioner ruled that Sevenoaks Council was guilty in not removing some Gypsies from land neighbouring the com-

plainant. They owned the land themselves and had been living on it (albeit without planning permission) before the house-dweller had bought her house. She was awarded compensation.

• In 1995 two families living in houses next to a new caravan site were awarded £400 to be paid by Cornwall County Council because of the effect on the view from their windows of the inadequate landscaping of the site.

The Public Order Act of 1986

One of the provisions of the Public Order Act increased pressure on unsited Gypsies, although it was introduced to deal with New Travellers. We deal elsewhere with other parts of the Act which concern incitement to racial hatred.

As a result of the confrontations between New Travellers and police in 1986 the Government decided to introduce new measures against trespass in the Public Order Bill during its passage through the House of Lords. The new clause was tabled on 26 September 1986. Four days later the Department of the Environment wrote to interested organisations 'consulting' them about the clause. They had less than a week to reply before the debate took place. The replies we have seen all protested but it was in vain. The new clause was added to the Bill.

Under the new provisions (Section 39 of the Act) a police officer could order trespassers to leave land without a court order if:

> (a) any of those persons has caused damage to property on the land or used threatening, abusive or insulting words or behaviour ... or (b) have between them brought twelve or more vehicles on to the land.

If they did not leave, any uniformed policeman could arrest them without a warrant.

When the debate reached the House of Commons, Gerald Kaufman, then spokesman for the Opposition, raised the question of Gypsies:

> Gypsies had better travel in small groups. As long as they travel with twelve caravans or fewer and behave themselves they will be all right. The moment they travel in groups of twelve or more, they will be in trouble.

Douglas Hogg, for the Government, replied:

> The right honourable gentleman (Mr Kaufman) belly-ached about Gypsies. The purpose of the new clause is not to harass innocent Gypsies. However, if Gypsies create the nuisance contemplated by the Bill, I see no reason why it should not be extended to cover them.

In fact, Gypsies had to travel in groups of less than six families as a caravan and a lorry count as *two* vehicles.

The Home Office wrote to a Gypsy organisation in February 1987:

> Neither the Government or the police have any wish to harass well-behaved Travellers … Highways were specifically excluded from the scope of the section so that Gypsies can stop on them.

So Gypsy families were encouraged by this law to stop on the edge of roads, with all the inherent dangers, rather than pull into a piece of unoccupied land.

This new legislation was soon in force. In April 1987 two families of Travellers stopped on a piece of parkland in Haringey. Because they had 'damaged' the surrounding fence when they took it down in order to get into the park, they came within the rules of the new Act. John W. as well as his wife, and Mrs M. in the second caravan were all three fined £40 and £10 costs.

The Criminal Justice and Public Order Act of 1994 (see below) strengthens the provisions on trespass.

The General Elections of 1987 and 1992

In the run up to the 1987 General Election, Conservative candidates in particular used the Gypsy issue to win votes. Christopher Murphy, MP for Welwyn-Hatfield, brought in a short bill entitled Gypsies (Control of Unauthorised Encampments) Act 1987 which would have *designated* the whole of England and Wales as an area where Gypsies could not stop and made outlaws at a stroke of some 4,000 families. Seven years later these suggestions were to be incorporated in legislation.

In March 1987 Peter Lilley (MP for St Albans) initiated a debate on Gypsy Caravan Sites. He wanted no more sites to be built in either Green Belt or residential areas as, he said, the majority of the public do not want to live 'cheek by jowl' with Gypsies. His suggestion was to put sites in out of the way rural areas. He talked too of an influx of a previously unheard of group called 'Irish didicois' who should not be classed as Gypsies and for whom no sites should be provided. Another MP, Sir Hugh Rossi, claimed in the debate that his constituents 'suffered horrendous problems because of an invasion of the area by so-called Gypsies'. During the 1987 election Conservative Party officials in Bradford were seen handing out stickers for cars bearing the message: Keep the Gypsies out – Vote Conservative. After protests the stickers were withdrawn.

It should be said that at local level there has been little difference between Labour and Conservative councillors in their attitude to providing sites for Gypsies. In Hackney, Labour man David Pollock lists (in his leaflet) achievements by De Beauvoir's remaining two Labour councillors to back his party's case. He said: 'Councillors Michael Barber and Carole Young ... have ensured the eviction of travellers'.

The new Government elected in 1987 had a fresh report compiled by Professor Wibberley. Its recommendations were similar to those of John Cripps. Published in 1986 they are still valid and we give below the most important:

- The definition of a Gypsy should be made more specific
- Better and more frequent counts of the numbers are needed.
- There must be a speeding up of the process of providing authorised local authority sites and a concerted attempt to increase the range and number of private sites.
- Some provision of transit sites, primarily for long-distance travellers.

The Government elected in 1987 did little in this matter. In view of the anti-Gypsy views expressed by many Government MPs during the General Election campaign, Gypsies may well have breathed a sigh of relief as any legislation might well have worsened their situation.

Nicholas Ridley summed up the situation in a Parliamentary Reply in February 1987 prior to the election, saying the Government has decided that there should be no amendment of the legislation at this stage.

Likewise, falling back on the need for more information, as had his predecessor in 1950: 'An early priority will be to examine how information on Gypsy numbers could be improved'. The Gypsy Sites Branch of the Department was to get a sixth member, attached to the Social

Research Division, who would carry out a research programme and supervise privatised research contracts.

By the time of the 1992 General Election, New Travellers were high on the political agenda. In his speech to the Conservative Conference before the election, Mr Major highlighted the need to control New Travellers and for more toilets on the motorways as priorities for the new government. This time action was taken, as we show below.

Department of the Environment Circular 1/94

As the Government's first step in a two-pronged attack upon the existing policies for Gypsies in January 1994 the Department of the Environment issued a circular (1/94) the main intentions of which were ' to provide that the planning system recognises the need for accommodation consistent with Gypsies' nomadic lifestyle; to reflect the importance of the plan-led nature of the planning system in relation to Gypsy site provision ...and to withdraw the previous guidance indicating that it may be necessary to accept the establishment of Gypsy sites in protected areas such as Green Belts.'

A circular represents advice from the Government which a local authority ignores at its peril. This circular has in practice made it more difficult to get permission for caravan sites, although it was issued at the same time as the Government was proclaiming as a policy that Gypsies should provide their own sites.

The second prong was to be the abolition of the 1968 Caravan Sites Act and the introduction of new penalties for trespass.

New Labour are keeping this circular in force. Miss Bird, a civil servant in the Department of Environment, stated soon after the 1997 election that 'there are no plans to withdraw the advice in circular 1/94 that Gypsy caravan sites are not normally regarded as being appropriate development in Green Belt areas'.

The circular advised local authorities to have a planning policy for Gypsies. A useful report prepared by Mark Wilson and supported by the Advisory Council for the Education of Romany and other Travellers (ACERT), published in 1998, found that 30 per cent of local authorities in England had no such policy. The majority of the others had criteria-based policies and the author identified sixty-three different criteria which were used in different places to judge whether a proposal for a private site might be granted. Nearly all criteria require a site to be neither adjacent to existing accommodation nor in the countryside, two contradictory requirements. Without exception the criteria require the site to be screened already or capable of screening, so that the caravans cannot be seen by cars or passing pedestrians. Other criteria included:

* the site must be flat (Lincoln City Council)
* the family has been resident in the district for five years (Canterbury)
* access to the site is not through existing housing areas (Carrick)
* the site must be capable of easy and regular supervision (East Lindsey)
* the site should be of a size to allow ready assimilation into the local community (Leominster)
* the proposals should result in acceptable smell impact (Mid Devon)
* sites are only permitted in areas which have traditionally been stopping points for Gypsies (Richmondshire).

ACERT has prepared a further report – on the result of applications for planning permission for private sites. A research report by Friends, Families and Travellers Support Group (FFT) in 1996 suggested that less than 10 per cent of initial planning applications by Gypsies were successful. Other surveys suggest the even lower figure of 4 per cent. This compares with 80 per cent of the total number of applications for any form of planning permission.

The courts have ruled in respect of Circular 1/94 that the personal circumstances of Gypsies must be considered. In the ongoing case of Marlene Ayres in South Gloucestershire, the Judge rejected the claim made on behalf of the Secretary of State that 'the effect of Circular 1/94 was to make the status of Gypsy irrelevant [and that] the mere fact of being a Gypsy in need of a site could not amount to a very special circumstance'.

In practice, to get permission in a Green Belt does require something special, for example, a large family and the absence of an official site or severely disabled children.

In another case (Rexworthy v. Secretary of State and Leominster D.C. 1998) Mr Malcolm Spence QC looked at the first sentence in paragraph 22 of Circular 1/94 which reads:

> As with any other planning applications, proposals for Gypsy sites should continue to be determined solely in relation to land use factors.

Mr Spence said this sentence was ineptly and ambiguously worded. Factors other than land use have to be considered, such as the lack of official sites in the area.

The Department of the Environment, Transport and the Regions (as it is now called) commented on this decision saying the sentence simply meant that applications by Gypsies should be determined without regard to any prejudice against them!

There may be an increase in Gypsies getting planning permission on appeal following Mr Spence's comment that personal circumstances have to be considered – which is indeed what another Government circular (PPG1) says.

A small step forward in helping Gypsies to get planning permission was a letter from the Department of the Environment to all local authorities in 1998 pointing out the need for a policy on Gypsies. It stated that the absence of such a policy could be a material consideration in favour of an Inspector granting planning permission on appeal. It will also be relevant in enforcement procedures against roadside camps.

The 1994 Criminal Justice and Public Order Act

The first step after the 1991 Election was the issuing of a joint press release by the Home Office and the Department of the Environment announcing the intention to reform the 1968 Caravan Sites Act. A consultation document was then issued and over a thousand replies were received, mostly opposing the idea of repealing the 1968 Caravan Sites Act. The Government pressed ahead however and – in spite of the opposition of the Labour and Liberal Democrats in the House of Commons and all-party opposition in the House of Lords – new measures were enacted as part of the 1994 Criminal Justice and Public Order Act (CJPOA).

The House of Lords tried to keep some of the provisions of the 1968 Caravan Sites Act in force for a further five years, and the Labour opposition in the Commons supported this. Peter Pike, their spokesman for Home Affairs said:

> The Government's proposals to repeal part of the Caravan Sites Act 1968 do not solve any problems but create more…What would be achieved by passing the Bill?…to do so would criminalise some Gypsies and increase homelessness; it would cause family breakdown and place added pressures on social and education services. It would certainly not solve any problems. Indeed it is our view that it would create more problems and improve nothing.

Lord Irvine, at the time Labour Party Spokesman on Home Affairs in the Lords, was most scathing about the government's proposals during the Report stage of the Bill on 11 July:

> There is humbug at the heart of the Government's policy …at the same time as they suggest that private site provision is the solution on which we should rely, they are making such provision more difficult by altering national planning policies.

Unfortunately, Lord Irvine has not been able to persuade his colleagues in the New Labour government to do anything about this humbug.

In the Act, the number of vehicles needed to commit 'collective' trespass was reduced to six, which means that a maximum of two families (two caravans and two towing vehicles) can stop together on roadside sites. The powers given by 'designation' under the 1968 Act to councils that had provided enough sites were made nation-wide and now apply to all caravans:

> If it appears to a local authority that persons are for the time being residing in a vehicle or vehicles within that authority's area (a) on any land forming part of a highway; (b) on any other unoccupied land or (c) on any occupied land without the consent of the occupier the authority may give a direction that those persons … are to leave the land and remove the vehicle or vehicles.

Not moving within a reasonable time after being asked to do so by the police or a local council then becomes a criminal offence.

In February 1995 in one of the first prosecutions under the new Act two Irish Traveller families were given twenty-four hours to get off private land by Tonbridge magistrates. This they did by moving to the other side of the road.

The new 1994 Act also repealed such parts as remained of those circulars which had encouraged tolerance both for unofficial and private sites. A new government circular in 1994 (18/94) was to ask councils to tolerate unofficial sites where these 'cause no nuisance'. (Tolerated roadside sites in this sense should be distinguished from the toleration of private sites which do not have planning permission). Previous guidance had been to tolerate illegal sites where there was no public site available.

One result of the new Act (section 80) was the repeal of the 1968 Caravan Sites Act and with it the duty to provide sites. This does not just mean that councils no longer need to build sites. It means that they can close the sites they have already built and, with the disappearance of the duty on councils to provide sites, the absence of a pitch will be of less weight in a defence against an accusation of trespass or an application for planning permission for a private site.

Sussex closed one of its sites and moved all the families into housing. Within a short space of time seven out of ten families had abandoned their houses and gone back on the road.

The number of pitches on council sites has gone down in recent years. During 1996 there was a net loss of sixteen pitches and between January 1997 and January 1998 a further decrease of thirty-four pitches. This last figure excludes forty-nine pitches which were transferred from council to private ownership.

The Local Government Commissioner since 1994

Since the repeal of the 1968 Caravan Sites Act in 1994, the involvement of the Local Government Ombudsman in Gypsy matters has been much reduced. Nevertheless, there follow some of the few examples.

Mr 'Andover' (the name given to him by the Ombudsman) bought some land in north-west Leicestershire but was refused planning permission. The Council then started enforcement proceedings against him for being in breach of planning law. With no immediate possibility of finding another piece of land Mr Andover reluctantly applied for housing as a homeless person. Under the Housing (Homeless Persons) Act someone living in a caravan is classed as homeless if they have nowhere legally to station the caravan. The council did not reply to his request. The Commissioner ruled that the Andovers would not be homeless until the Council was about to evict them and that they should be informed officially of this situation. It was further ruled that they should be paid £350 to compensate for the delay in informing them of their position.

In 1995 Hackney Council decided to use its powers under the 1960 Caravan Sites Act to build a new permanent site for Travellers and move them from their existing site (which had been provided under the 1968 Caravan Sites Act). Discussions within the Council on building this site dragged on and finally the Travellers were evicted from their original site and resited on a third temporary site which had no facilities. There was no electricity and one tap. Six chemical toilets were provided to be shared by fifteen families (plus two which were there without permission). Each family could only have one caravan, which meant older boys had to sleep with younger children of both sexes. The Commissioner ruled that each of the fifteen families who were official tenants should be paid £250 to compensate for having to live in these unsatisfactory conditions.

In the same year Bedford Borough Council was recommended to pay £750 to Gypsy families who had earlier been left without facilities while waiting to be relocated on a new site.

On the other hand in 1995 Humberside County Council was ordered to pay £250 compensation to the neighbours of an unofficial site in Cleethorpes for the 'nuisance' they had suffered from the presence of the Gypsies.

Department of the Environment Circular 18/94

The circular issued following the Criminal Justice Act (Department of the Environment Circular 18/94) urged tolerance in eviction policies in respect of Gypsies and drew attention to the wider obligations authorities might have to Gypsies and Travellers under other legislation concerning homelessness and children. Two High Court judgements in 1995 emphasised that local authorities could not evict Gypsies without making proper enquiries concerning the health and welfare of the persons to be evicted.

Mr Justice Sedley in cases heard at the same time in August (R v. Lincolnshire CC ex parte Atkinson, R v. Wealden DC ex parte Wales and Stratford) ruled:

> The material considerations in Circular 18/94 are considerations of common humanity, none of which can be ignored when dealing with one of the most fundamental human rights, the need for shelter with at least a modicum of security.

Later the same year, Mr Justice Latham dealt with a similar case where Kerrier District Council was seeking to evict Catherine Uzzell and other New Travellers from a highways materials storage depot where they had been living, by the issuing of an enforcement notice. He referred to an oft-quoted statement by Lord Scarman during a planning case which did not involve caravans:

> It would be inhuman to exclude from the control of our environment the human factor. The human factor is always present of course indirectly in the background to the consideration of the character of land use. It can, however, and sometimes should be given direct effect as an exceptional or special circumstance.

In this particular case, however, Mr Justice Latham concluded that the human factor had been adequately considered and that the Council was justified in evicting the Travellers. The Wealden case, as it is usually referred to, will slow down but not stop the process of evictions under the Criminal Justice Act.

It is worrying that Lord Scarman's dictum has recently been cited by the opposition to the granting of planning permission to a private Gypsy site in Bedfordshire. It was argued that the objections of many villagers to the site were a human factor that had to be considered.

The obligation to make welfare enquiries does not apply to the police using section 61 of the Criminal Justice and Public Order Act of 1994 to evict caravan dwellers. There is, however, a Home Office circular (45/1994) which says that police officers 'may wish to take account of the presence of elderly persons, invalids, pregnant women and children'.

In practice, the police evict more quickly than the local authorities and on at least one occasion, in Grantham, 1998, have used CS gas on Travellers during an eviction.

Local authorities have evolved various strategies for dealing with unauthorised encampments. Somerset County Council, for example, has set up a Travellers Policy Review Panel with representatives of the district and parish councils, landowners, the National Farmers Union, religious bodies and the Travellers themselves. Essex, Cambridgeshire and other councils have evolved Gypsy codes.

Doncaster has a very positive statement of policy in relation to unauthorised Gypsy and Traveller encampments, including the statements:

> 3. The Council will at all times act in a humane and compassionate fashion.
> 6. Gypsies will not be moved unnecessarily from place to place

On the negative side, Northampton has encouraged landowners to take protection measures (ditches, boulders) to stop illegal encampments on their land. A local authority now has the power to take action against trespassers on private land but Northampton has told landowners that it will not continue to take action on behalf of a private landowner if protection works are not undertaken.

1997 – New Labour in Government

Gypsies and New Travellers were not a national issue in the 1997 General Election, although in the campaign leading to county council elections held on the same day some candidates saw the subject as sufficiently important to include it in their manifestos. Rodney Bass, a bank executive standing for election to Essex County Council as a Conservative, declared:

> I believe that Essex County Council should reduce spending on social services and stop treating hooligans with kid gloves and giving special favours to Gypsies.

In spite of its opposition to the repeal of the 1968 Caravan Sites Act there was no Labour manifesto pledge to reintroduce it, and Gypsies and Travellers were not seen as a priority by the new Government. With one eye already fixed on winning the next election, there were few votes to be won – and many to be lost – over this issue.

As in other areas, the new Government was to follow the policy of the previous Conservative government with Gypsies remaining the

responsibility of the Homelessness and Housing Management Section at
Eland House. In a somewhat belated response to a letter sent from a
Gypsy organisation to the Minister of State, Hilary Armstrong, a civil
servant – Rob John at the Department of the Environment, Transport
and the Regions – wrote on August 11th 1997:

> Current policy is as set out in Department of the Environment Circulars
> 1/94 'Gypsy Sites and Planning' and 18/84 'Gypsy Sites Policy and
> Unauthorised Camping'.

In other words, there was to be no change.

In November that same year, Hilary Armstrong wrote to the Editor of
the *Bristol Evening Post* (in response to articles in that paper):

> We have no plans to make the law harsher. Even if we were persuaded it
> was the right course, harsher treatment may bring the UK government
> into conflict with both the domestic courts and the European Court of
> Human Rights. We are working to improve best practice by local authori-
> ties in their dealings with travellers... research is being done now and the
> best practice advice will be out next spring.

Publication of the advice (mentioned above) was in fact delayed till the
following autumn (1998) and introduced to the public by Nick
Raynsford, Parliamentary Under-Secretary of State at the Department of
the Environment, Transport and the Regions in a speech in Leicester in
October 1998. He was clear about what the Government would not do:

> We have thought hard about whether to return to the position in the
> Caravan Sites Act of 1968 and whether to return to the days of mandato-
> ry municipal site provisions. And we have concluded that would be a
> retrograde step.

He rejected the suggestion of the Local Government Association that the
Government should set quotas for public site provision in each locality
and the demand of Gypsies for the advice in Circular 1/94 to be relaxed
to aid the development of private sites.

As for planning policy: 'We will not be making any changes to the
policy set out in Circular 1/94' declared Mr Raynsford, although he did
draw attention to the letter that the Department had written to Chief
Planning Officers earlier in the year telling them that the Government
expects them to include 'clear and realistic' policies to meet the needs of

Gypsies wanting to provide their own sites. In this keynote speech the Minister suggested that some of the £7 million spent annually by local authorities on evictions could be used to provide temporary sites or transit pitches.

The Code of Good Practice

The repeal of the 1968 Caravan Sites Act in autumn 1994 left, according to government figures, nearly 3,000 families still on the roadside. There were no permanent or transit pitches available for them on official sites. The total number of families on the roadside has not changed since then, as the formation of new households has outstripped the provision of new legal pitches. Under the harsh provisions of the 1994 Criminal Justice and Public Order Act these Gypsies became virtually outlaws. In a half-hearted attempt to regularise their position, the Government issued circular 18/94 (see above).

This was followed by some individual counties and districts producing their own 'Gypsy codes'. These varied but the one adopted by Essex in February 1995 is a typical example:

> Subject to the satisfactory assessment of the following factors, Essex authorities will not normally pursue an order for the removal of vehicles from any land on which they are stationed for a period of between 14 and 28 days ...
>
> 2. The maximum number of caravans normally acceptable will be three caravans in any one group ...
>
> 5. The minimum acceptable distance between groups of Travellers shall normally be half a mile ...
>
> 7. No fires shall be lit on any land.

In most parts of England, nomadic Gypsies find it hard to stop anywhere. As the tenant of an official site in south London recounted in 1998:

> One fellow pulled off the site about two weeks ago. He wanted to work his way down to Dover and then cross to France. He came back because he couldn't stop anywhere and he got fed up with people keeping on to him [to move]. So he came back here to the site and went back on the dole.

A Romany family stopped on private land in Wadebridge, Cornwall, in 1998. Immediately the local police turned up with video and still cameras and began photographing the Gypsies and their vehicles. They served a direction under section 61 of the CJPO and told the family to move by the evening. The family had wanted to spend three weeks in Cornwall but on hearing the risk that their caravans and vehicles could be impounded, they left the same day.

Following research by the School of Public Policy at the University of Birmingham, commissioned by the previous government. the Labour Government has issued a Guide to Good Practice entitled *Managing Unauthorised Camping.* The Research Report itself felt that 'a range of site provision was needed in order to reduce the scale of unauthorised encampment and make rapid and firm action to tackle it more justifiable'. Extracts from the Guide itself are given below but the whole is essential reading for anyone involved with unauthorised sites:

- Local authorities should have an overall strategy towards Gypsy and Traveller issues, including needs assessment, site provision and service provision, as well as eviction policies, which should be developed with the local police force.
- All local authorities should seriously consider identifying 'acceptable' temporary stopping places.
- Where agencies or contractors are employed [for forced evictions], their proper behaviour must always be checked. Violence and avoidable damage to vehicles or other Gypsy and Traveller possessions is unacceptable.

The Government's Guide was the first step by the new Labour Government, elected in 1997, to intervene in the Gypsy and Traveller field. Even with these local and national codes, Gypsy families are still having difficulty in finding stopping places.

6

New Travellers

There is a need to travel …
There is a need to squat   There is a need for protest
There is a need for open spaces   There is a need to celebrate
There is a need for community   There is a need for tolerance
There is a need TO BE HEARD   STOP the Criminal *IN*Justice Act

(From a poster used by the Freedom Network (Brixton) to advertise the implications of the Criminal Justice and Public Order Act, 1994.)

Definitions and labels

As a New Traveller put it:

> There are as many different types of Travellers as there are people in society. Just face it, you can't put us in a box – we're all different. We don't all think the same way and we don't all behave the same way.

Despite the words and protests of New Travellers themselves, the common perception held by many people in the UK is that they fundamentally *are* in the one box: they think, behave, dress and roam about the country as a homogenous entity. It is because of this association that New Travellers have sometimes been talked about in terms of a 'plague' or a 'disease', 'descending like locusts' on an area. They are, in a sense, regarded as the new 'enemy within'.

The term 'New Age Traveller' has often been applied very loosely and without any real critical thought by the media to anyone of a certain appearance and demeanour. Stereotypically, in the 1980s and 1990s, the image presented to the tabloid reader was someone with lengthy dreadlocks, a variety of body-piercings, home-made tattoos, torn and battered army surplus clothing and the essential requirements of a 'ram-shackle' bus and a dog-on-a-string. The can of special brew (very strong lager) was also usually mentioned. Such an image, whilst not entirely unknown, is largely a stereotype. It really is not this simple and requires more critical thought and analysis.

It is certainly true that the definition of the term 'New Age Traveller' has widened in recent years to include a whole plethora of individuals who would not be happy to find themselves labelled as 'New Age Travellers'. Other colourful terms that have been used in place of 'New Age' Traveller include: medieval brigands (as Douglas Hurd once famously called them when he was Home Secretary in the mid-1980s), crusties, soap-dodgers, brew-crew, giro-Gypsies, drongos and plain old 'sponging scum'. These labels do give a sense of the fear and loathing that is held by the many against a few. It tells us, I would argue, a lot about those doing the labelling and not much about those being labelled. The contempt does not end with just a name: as with Gypsies New Travellers have had to endure both the romanticisation and demonisation of their culture and lifestyle. The 'freedom' is envied whilst the 'dirt and squalor' is loathed. From 'high-culture' academics who patronise them with overtly abstract and theoretical ideas about them being 'tourists on holiday from modernity' to the more blunt 'low-culture' accusations from the tabloid press of being idle, dirty, feckless drug-addicts, New Travellers have rarely been given a fair press. Perhaps one indication of who the New Travellers might really be comes from one Traveller called Offshore:

> We are just like the hippies of the 1960s but while they were giving it all 'peace and love' we now say 'peace and love… but just don't push it…' you know what I mean?

It would seem then that to at least some New Travellers in the 1990s, an earlier ethos and lifestyle is being remembered and drawn upon but at the same time it has a new spin on it to indicate a healthy scepticism and distance from those who would seek to attack the culture they adhere to. Some groups of Travellers still make significant efforts to adopt aspects of Native American life with status accorded to 'healers', 'elders', 'scribes' and 'matriarchs' but unlike the original hippies the modern day New Traveller is no pushover, rendered passive by Eastern spiritualism and tinted glasses. If kicked, they now kick back: and they have had to in recent years as will be shown below.

Origins and early history

The origins and history of New Travellers in Britain are easier to trace than those of the Gypsies. A written history exists alongside the oral one. The collective effort *A Time to Travel*? is a good example of such a book which provides us with a clear record of what was going on in the 1970s and 1980s New Traveller communities. Likewise, George McKay's recent book, *Senseless Acts of Beauty* gives a vivid account of the early festival scene in Britain and how important the New Traveller contribution to these events was. Perhaps the best book to date though is the one that lets New Travellers tell it like it is themselves. With only minimal editing, Lowe and Shaw's book *Travellers: Voices of the New Age Nomads* lets a group of New Travellers tell their story and it gives the reader an insight into the highs and many lows of living a New Traveller lifestyle in contemporary Britain.

With the emergence of the 1960s counter-culture movement (or 'scene' to use the terminology of the time) a number of mainly inner-city house-dwellers in the UK started to live in modified caravans and buses and travel up and down the country in search of work, stopping places and music festivals. The main areas where New Travellers went to included parts of Wales and the West Country. There was a good supply of casual work here and the climate was quite hospitable for outdoor living. Scotland and Ireland were also popular locations for some English New Travellers who were seeking to escape the pressures of modern life in England. During my own research, I met groups of New Travellers in the north of Scotland who suggested to me they were up north in an effort to shake-off heroin addiction, debts and to lead a more 'sorted' or peaceful life in the beauty and tranquillity of the Highlands. A number of these individuals moved on to the road for mainly economic reasons, whilst others changed accommodation and lifestyle due to their frustration and anger at what was happening in the inner-cities.

The initial New Traveller subculture based itself around a growing summer network of open air festivals and gatherings armed with an ideology of spiritualism, peace, and ecological respect. The early 1970s saw the first Glastonbury Free Festival and a summer solstice celebration at Stonehenge. Later on in this decade, the numbers adopting such a nomadic lifestyle grew, as did the number of festival events. By the mid-1970s there was a full diary from June till about September. A festival economy was starting to take-off and flourish. This growth occurred despite the harassment that New Travellers were receiving from concerned local residents, landowner groups, the press and the police. The free festival (economic) circuit was becoming too big to go unnoticed by the powers that be. Stonehenge alone was lasting a good couple of months. 'It was anarchy in action and it worked!' as Mo Lodge, one Traveller who was interviewed for the Morris brothers' Channel 4 documentary film *Operation Solstice* in 1991, declared. She was right. New Travellers were able to make enough money over the summer festival months to fund the winter shut-down and park-up. By crushing the festival circuit, the government of the day merely forced a large number of people to claim social security who otherwise were quite happy not claiming and making their own money.

Numbers

By the early to mid-1980s the number of people living a nomadic lifestyle in this way had grown to several thousand and this started to cause the government, from their perspective, a few problems. Estimates of numbers in the 'peace convoy' at this time ranged from 5,000 to 50,000. However, no one source could claim an accurate figure. Police figures came in at around the 7,000 to 8,000 mark whilst some organisations working with Travellers (such as the Save The Children Fund) suggested figures nearly five times as much. We would suggest that the 1999 figure stands at about 15,000. This figure includes those New Travellers living on boats but not those who may choose to spend winter in houses.

The 'Battle of the Beanfield' and beyond

Although there had been previous skirmishes between the police and New Travellers at Nostell Priory near Wakefield and at the famous Rainbow Village in Molesworth, it has been the infamous incident not far from Stonehenge in June 1985 that prompted the government to introduce measures in the 1986 Public Order Act (section 13: the so-called 'hippy' clause) to tighten up laws on trespass. This incident, which has come to be known as the *Battle of the Beanfield*, saw many Travellers and their movable homes being attacked by the police and certainly represents something of a watershed in the history of conflict between the police and New Travellers in Britain. However, it was less of a battle and more of a one-sided massacre. It should be noted, of course, that in marking out one event as a 'watershed' in any group's history is to simplify things too much. This said, it has been perceived by many as being a very significant event and it was. For example, it has been remembered vividly in a song by the Brighton-based folk-rock group *The Levellers* and has become something of an anthem in the folklore of New Travellers. The lyrics tell the story without compromise:

Battle of the Beanfield

I thought I heard someone calling me
I've seen the pictures on TV
And I made up my mind that I'd go and see
With my own eyes

It didn't take too long to hitch a ride
With a guy going South to start a new life
Past the place where my friend died
Two years ago

Down the [A] 303 at the end of the road
Flashing lights – exclusion zones
And it made me think it's not just the stones
That they're guarding

(chorus)
Hey hey, can't you see
There's nothing here that you could call free
They're getting their kicks
Laughing at you and me

As the sun rose on the beanfield
They came like wolf on the fold
And they didn't give a warning
They took their bloody toll

I see a pregnant woman
Lying in blood of her own
I see her children crying
As the police tore apart her home

And no they didn't need a reason
It's what your votes condone
It seems they were committing treason
By trying to live on the road.

(reproduced with kind permission.)

In the year that the Public Order Act 1986 was passed, a similar incident to that at the Beanfield occurred at Stoney Cross in the New Forest. The police got their opportunity to test out the new measures to full effect. The use of five to fifteen mile exclusion zones were now routine in areas such as Stonehenge and Glastonbury in an attempt to keep New Travellers away from the area. Indeed, as well as their nomadism being a point of conflict with sedentary society it is also their capacity to stay in certain areas that causes tension and anxiety for locals: disease, drugs and debauchery may just take root, given the chance!

The next generation: in search of an identity?

In the late 1980s and early 1990s a significant change occurred in the demography and composition of the New Traveller community. A number of young people from the cities who were being squeezed by Conservative social policies opted to take to the road. For many there was little choice in the matter due to the tightening of eligibility for social security benefits and a lack of affordable accommodation. Sections of the 1986 Social Security Act, which were implemented in 1988, meant that most 16 and 17 year-olds were denied benefit and it is no coincidence that from this point onwards there was a significant increase in the numbers of young people adopting a nomadic way of life. Similarly, changes in housing legislation around this time had led to

Laura, Jim and Sid with their new home; *photograph by Alan Dearling*

a lack of affordable accommodation and this also led to increasing numbers of both young and old New Travellers.

These young unemployed people living in cities, who had been denied benefit, opted to become 'New Age Travellers' rather than just being young, unemployed, penniless and homeless. Such economic refugees, if that is an appropriate phrase, became a part of a growing population that was now starting to reproduce itself so that first and second generations of New Travellers were now not so uncommon. Arguably, a new 'ethnic' culture was emerging, although the legal system did not recognise this in terms of sites legislation.

It should be made clear at this point that not all New Travellers fit the above description as unemployed refugees from the city. The current population travelling in caravans and buses – not to mention canal boats – also includes students, as well as financially self-supporting craftspeople, musicians, artists, writers, photographers, builders and mechanics. They come from choice seeking the freedom and the community spirit of the open road.

Elements of this younger generation of New Travellers, whilst to a certain extent respecting and admiring the 1960s and 1970s hippies make it quite clear that they are different in a number of respects, including philosophy and outlook. This is the point that Offshore was making in his earlier quote. To many, both within the New Traveller community and those outside it, the older generation were to be labelled as 'crusties' or 'the brew-crew'. Such terms were used largely due to their appearance and actions, revelling in the stereotypes mentioned above and often 'out to lunch' (intoxicated) on special brew lager (hence the nickname 'brew-crew'). In other words, they became a minority within a minority group that it was acceptable to fear, loathe, vilify and generally blame.

'Operation Snapshot'

One reaction of the state to this growth in New Traveller numbers during the 1980s and 1990s was to keep a check on who was moving where, when and in what vehicle. It represented a classic piece of police monitoring and surveillance and it was known as Operation Snapshot. This police effort, located at bases in Wiltshire and Cumbria, aimed to gather information and establish a computer database on what the police regarded as the hard-core New Travellers. The intelligence units documented names, nicknames, known acquaintances, details on type of accommodation and other information deemed to be of use in keeping one step ahead of their movements. A profile was built up of the various free festival dates and who was most likely to be behind the organisation of the various events.

This information, and that of the similar Operation Nomad, despite the Data Protection Act of 1984, has been shared amongst the various agencies of the state, especially between the police, the Post Office and the DSS. Indeed, it was the 'wanton' claiming of social security benefits by New Travellers that the media and politicians primarily picked up on in their headlines and speeches. Peter Lilley, at the Conservative Party conference in 1992, likened New Travellers to locusts: they descend to demand benefits with menace. Indeed, New Travellers served an important political purpose here as Lilley, on the strength of anti-New Traveller sentiments, was able to push through draconian changes to existing social security legislation that was to impact on not just New

Protestors like these occupying housing in the path of the planned M11 route in Leytonstoe/Leytonstonia in 1994 have began to gain support from middle England; *photographs by Colin Clark*

Travellers but so-called bogus asylum seekers, single mothers and essentially anyone who was young, single and unemployed. The net had been tightened thanks to the public hatred directed at New Travellers.

The Criminal Justice Act 1994 and New Travellers

Almost a decade on from the 'Battle of the Beanfield', the 1994 Criminal Justice and Public Act was passed which further tightened up the laws on trespass and made a nomadic lifestyle a criminal activity. The sections of this Act (61-80) that were introduced relating to Gypsies as well as to New Travellers were again influenced by events a year or so earlier. In the summer of 1992 (the 'second summer of love' according to some cultural commentators) an outdoor event in the Malvern Hills, at Castlemorton, saw some 20,000 to 40,000 New Travellers, ravers and local youths get together to hold an impromptu gathering. The government of the day was determined, this time, to make sure such a large assembly never happened again on British soil and the relevant sections of the CJPOA 1994 began to be drawn up. With the Labour Party abstaining on the votes, the Bill eventually became an Act in November 1994.

After the Criminal Justice Act 1994

The impact of the CJPOA 1994 and the earlier Public Order Act of 1986 on the British New Traveller communities has been quite profound. The legislation accentuated a trend which, for some years now, has seen some New Travellers migrating to other parts of Europe. Preferred locations seem to include Spain, Portugal, France and Sweden. A few New Travellers have even made it as far as South Africa and Goa in India. The one common message that is filtering back to the UK from these New Travellers who are abroad is that of a much more relaxed attitude towards them from both local people and officialdom. Certainly this is reflected in what some New Travellers wrote for the recent Alan Dearling collection *No Boundaries* (1998). Others have chosen to stay in Britain and, for the time being, park-up their bus where they can and see what the future holds. Others still have decided, quite bravely, to take on the legislation, keep at it and continue to pursue a nomadic way of life. To dismiss such individuals as drop-outs and idle scroungers blatantly ignores the determination and resilience that drives them on to lead the way of life that they are drawn to, for whatever reason.

Education

Derek Hawes and Barbara Perez in their book *The Gypsy and the State* (1996) suggest that the development of education policies concerned with the needs of Gypsies and other Travellers can be divided into at least three historical periods. The 'early years' covers the period from 1902 until the passing of the Education Act of 1944, the 'voluntary initiatives' period is considered to be the 1960s and 1970s and the 'multi-cultural and co-ordinated service' period takes us into the 1980s and 1990s. The situation of New Travellers in relation to state education policies designed for Travellers does not fall so easily into the three-period model. However, Section 36 of the 1944 Education Act does state:

> Parents are obliged to ensure that their child receives efficient full-time education suitable to the child's age, aptitude, or any special educational needs he or she may have, while of compulsory school age.

This 'full-time education' does not have to take place in a state school of course. The Act also goes on to say that the child must be 'receiving efficient full-time education ... either by regular attendance at school or otherwise'.

Many New Travellers who are parents have picked up on the 'or otherwise'. The parents do largely appreciate the need for some degree of state schooling, especially in relation to basic skills and literacy, exams and gaining qualifications. However, equally, if not more impor-tant to many parents, is the fact that their children should be able to 'learn through life' and possess a number of practical skills in living the lifestyle of a nomad: e.g. wooding, cleaning and maintenance of vehicles and the home, cooking, collecting kindling and picking fruit and veg-etables. In other words, children's education is opened up to reflect their experiences of living on a site and travelling with their parents and friends. Children learn a great deal from being close to and working

with adults as they go about their daily routines. Play amongst younger
children also reflects this, e.g. playing with toy trucks and transforming
them into 'homes' or 'scrapping' them when they are beyond repair. The
environment and nature are also topics that are on the curriculum.

There is a healthy scepticism and questioning of the types of state
education services that are available amongst many New Traveller communities. This scepticism has been endorsed, to some extent, by Arthur
Ivatts, Consultant to OFSTED, with responsibility for Traveller
Education:

> The New Traveller communities have introduced the rare concept of ask-
> ing new and different questions about education.... Questions such as
> what are we raising standards for? Who is driving this? Will it result in
> greater wealth? How will this wealth be distributed? Who will be
> accountable? Will it improve children's lives or is it about competing
> with the Pacific Rim? Will it increase the spiritual quality of life?

Whilst nearly all New Traveller parents do ask these questions that
Arthur Ivatts mentions above, it is true that for many it is important that
their children receive a sound secondary education and get some qualifications. Interestingly, the reverse seems to be true for primary level children who live on sites with their parents. Home education is seen by
many parents as a preferred option at this level of education. For many
Romany Gypsy parents this is the 'wrong way round'. many Gypsies are
keen that their children get to enjoy the benefits of a primary school
education. At eleven or twelve the children generally come out of the
state system to enjoy the education offered to them by family and
friends. They become adults and start to fully acquire the skills and
knowledge it requires to be a good Traveller.

In England and Wales a variety of voluntary and statutory groups
exist to enable New Traveller children and parents to access educational
opportunities. At the state level, Traveller Education Services (TES) and
the Education Welfare Services (EWS) throughout the country work to
ensure that New Travellers have increased opportunity to get support
from teachers and local schools where this is possible or appropriate.
Flexibility in local education services is the ideal situation although this
is not often seen to be the case from reports that have been given to the
Traveller School Charity (TSC), whose work will be outlined more fully
below as it is one of the main voluntary Charity groups working with

New Traveller children. Other organisations, such as the Children's Society and Friends, Families and Travellers Support Group, work to a similar remit with the general aim to meet the varied needs of Traveller children in their different environments and to facilitate learning.

The next section details the history and work of the Traveller School Charity which has perhaps done more than any other organisation or agency to promote and meet the educational needs of New Traveller children who live nomadically with their parents. For a much fuller account of New Traveller education and the work of TSC please consult the books by Earle and Dearling in the bibliography.

The Traveller School Charity

The Traveller School Charity (TSC), established in 1984 as a self-help organisation to 'advance the education and training of children', is one of the most well-known groups working with children whose parents follow a nomadic way of life. The management and staff of TSC have all at some point in time been New Travellers and many still live a nomadic existence. This fact gives TSC teachers a good degree of understanding when it comes to what New Traveller children and their parents are looking for in terms of an education.

It was around 1986-87 that things progressed for TSC and eventually, after various fund campaigns, the Skool Bus was purchased and in 1988 it was mobile and travelling to various New Traveller sites in England and Wales. It was in this year that TSC received its charity status which helped in terms of making applications for funding. By 1989 and 1990 running the bus and stocking it with necessary educational materials and equipment was becoming expensive. Also, as it was the only mobile resource, it was not managing to get to as many sites as the staff would have wanted it to. Those New Travellers who got a visit were full of praise for it, but equally those who did not were rather disgruntled about the situation.

In 1990 Fiona Earle joined TSC as a teacher and was using the bus as a mobile classroom. However, TSC was, by now, more than the bus and to some within the charity it was a problem, rather than a solution to the needs of educating New Traveller children on sites. Part of this problem was the sheer effort and cost it was taking to maintain and move the bus

The Traveller School Charity's Geodesic Dome school; *photograph by Alan Dearling*

to various sites. Also, with increasing police pressure, smaller New Traveller sites were becoming the norm rather than the larger ones. This just added to a host of practical problems in meeting needs.

In 1991 Fiona Earle was using a smaller and more mobile caravan as a classroom. This was towed by her own vehicle. However, just a couple of years later, the direction of TSC was uncertain and the future looked bleak. Indeed, from about 1993 to 1995 TSC was at a low point, and the bus was gone and disputes and internal rifts looked to be breaking the charity apart.

Not all was lost though. 1996 represented something of a new start for the TSC and new funding opportunities and projects began to develop and enthusiasm was returning to those within TSC. To date, the achievements and work of TSC since 1996 have been many and illustrate how important its existence is for New Traveller children outside the state schooling system. In the past couple of years it has taken on more teachers and has organised conferences and kids camps as well as on-site education in tents. Though TSC has had a shaky history, its future seems bright and those involved in the charity seem confident about continuing to meet the needs of New Traveller children who are outside the state education system.

Health

As Derek Hawes in his recent report on Gypsy and Traveller health wrote:

> New Travellers are considerably more aware of the services they can get than traditional families and are capable of being more assertive in dealing with bureaucracy. Young mothers will often return to settled living during pregnancy, in order to ensure good antenatal care and subsequent support. It was said by respondents that having children is a sure means of obtaining whatever services the family may need. Some reported that they retain registration with a GP in their original place of domicile.

Following a nomadic lifestyle has many implications for how basic public services are accessed, delivered and taken-up. This is especially true when it comes to the National Health Service (NHS). There are problems encountered by New Travellers in registering with a GP or getting treatment at a hospital, no matter how aware and assertive they may be, as Derek Hawes implies above.

For some New Travellers, traditional or standard health services such as those provided through the NHS system are ones that are either simply 'out of reach' or to be avoided as much as possible. This rejection, whether based on ideology or negative experiences in the past, leads some to embrace a more holistic approach to healthcare which takes in such 'alternative' practices as herbalism or homeopathy. There are various examples of men, women and children being refused registration with a GP on the basis of 'transient' status in the local area. Likewise, since the implementation of GP fundholding in 1991, the situation has been reported as getting even worse for New Travellers (and many other sections of the population) when attempting to register. As well as being too transient they are also too expensive. GPs have no financial 'carrot' to register patients who will not help the practice achieve its performance targets: expensive patients are a liability. Such examples of exclusion include the cases of pregnant women who have been refused ante-natal care from GPs. In situations like this it seems the preferred option is to find a relatively secure and safe stopping place and try to build up good relationships with sympathetic local midwives and health visitors.

New Travellers have a pragmatic approach to health care. Often, the approach that is taken will include using the NHS and 'alternative' health care methods simultaneously. As with most patients, this is never a passive exercise and some form of control over the situation is desired. For example, like many Gypsies, some New Travellers tend to rely on the nearest Accident and Emergency department for immediate treatment for one particular injury or complaint. This is perhaps viewed by some as not being an ideal solution or encouraging in terms of preventative medical care, but for the New Traveller or Gypsy it is the NHS doing its job: free health care at the point of use (and without much paperwork).

It is certainly true that some New Travellers do retain a GP where they have a more permanent residence. This is also the case for those who choose to park-up over the winter months. Needless to say, the chances of a successful registration with a GP and a better quality of health care are improved when a fixed address can be given. Health records can be established and allow for a continuity of care that more nomadic New Travellers may not have access to.

The 1997 report by Derek Hawes *Gypsies, Travellers and the Health Service* contends that '... from the evidence of health visitors and others, the levels of poor health, of child neglect, and in some cases, of drug and alcohol abuse, are serious among New Travellers...'

This raises several questions. It would be interesting to know whether these 'serious' levels of health, child neglect and drug/alcohol abuse are also applicable to the settled population (and who the 'others' are that Hawes speaks of). It is unhelpful to suggest that serious issues such as child neglect or drug/alcohol misuse are endemic within New Traveller communities. To do so, as Thomas Acton has pointed out in an online review of the study, is to pathologise such communities and ignore wider environmental issues. The status of being a Traveller is not a health variable in its own right. Likewise, when Hawes states that some New Travellers have a 'widespread illicit drug dependency' and are involved in a 'criminal subculture' he provides no supporting evidence to substantiate these claims. Gross generalisations abound in this report about the health and general lifestyle of New Travellers and Gypsies and it does little to smooth the path towards such groups having access to effective and appropriate healthcare.

On the other hand, according to the pamphlet New nomadic groups by Vicki Stangroome on New Travellers and healthcare, hard drug use by New Travellers is relatively rare (especially heroin) and is largely not tolerated on sites. She also argues that within the communities there are internal divisions regarding what is and what is not acceptable behaviour on sites. For example, where a site has a lot of families with children, unwritten rules develop amongst those on the site regarding what kinds of behaviour are tolerated and not tolerated. People coming onto the site may be informed of the 'code of conduct' and asked to abide by it and respect it. Extreme anti-social drinking or using needles to inject drugs intravenously are the kinds of behaviour that are as unacceptable to many New Travellers groups as they are to settled communities. It is disingenuous and a fallacy to portray New Travellers as alcohol-fuelled heroin addicts who have no interest in their own or their children's health. This is a picture that is far from the truth and the emphasis should be on improving access to GPs and other forms of healthcare for Travellers rather than merely blaming the sick for their own ill-health.

Work

Although the image of New Travellers is one that often sees them castigated as dole scroungers, many of them do, of course, work for a living and have many skills and trades. Skills can be traded with others on-site and with residents of other sites in the near area. They can also be used in the local area more generally amongst the settled population on a cash or exchange basis.

Like Gypsies, most New Travellers prefer being self-employed regarding work. The reasons for this are very similar to why Gypsies prefer self-employment: it gives them the power to control their own working agenda and set their own pace, price and type of job undertaken. Again, like Gypsies, the recommendation for a good job done spreads far and wide.

The range of trades followed by New Travellers is as varied as amongst the settled population. These include mechanics, welders, joiners and electricians. As well as those following particular trades, there are some New Travellers with qualifications in other areas. There are a number of professional occupations that, with some flexibility and understanding from clients, lend themselves to being nomadic: e.g. teachers, health visitors, journalists, researchers, photographers. Also, some New Travellers have successfully accessed state services or grants in helping to get a prospective business off the ground, such as the Princes Trust or some of the European funds.

There are many other types of work associated with New Travellers. One is craft work, that is making jewellery, pottery, clothes and the like. Such items can be made during the winter park-up (from about September to March) and sold during the summer period at festivals and other gatherings and fairs.

Busking at festivals, as well as in town centres, is also a method of supplementing an income. Likewise, begging and selling the street magazine The Big Issue are other sources of income. In the 1980s and early 1990s some of the larger festivals used to employ squads of New Travellers to maintain or organise a specific area (e.g., the gate, fencing, bin duty, etc.). This did happen at Glastonbury but during the late 1980s and early 1990s there was trouble between Michael Eavis, the landowner and festival organiser, and some New Travellers and the squad system was quickly ended. As well as official festivals there are also the unofficial gatherings (such as Letham in Angus, Scotland) where money is to be made from local settled 'customers' who come to listen to the sound systems and bands and to dance and get merry.

New Traveller kids particularly enjoy the fruit-picking season as young and nimble fingers tend to make much more money at the strawberry and raspberry picking than older ones (i.e. their parents). Again, this equally applies to Gypsy children.

Entertaining is a good way of earning a living too; circus skills (juggling, stilts, fire-breathing. etc.) can be quite in demand, especially in continental Europe. One such group was paid by the French government to run a nomadic circus on the south-coast and got a good price for their highly valued and skilled services!

As with Irish Travellers, scrapping (or recycling as it is now known) has also provided a means to an income. But recently, due to falling prices and changing government regulations on the types of vehicles that can be used for scrapping, many Travellers (both New and traditional) have been forced to turn from this occupation to others. Nonetheless, in urban areas such as London, Manchester and Glasgow, many groups are still involved in the industry.

Some New Travellers do hold down what we might term for want of a better expression 'normal jobs' (or 'wage labour') but the lack of a fixed address – as for homeless people – can make this difficult. Prejudice is encountered and employers can be reluctant to take on someone who gives their address as: the bus, c/o the lay-by near Gateshead.

In academic debates about 'flexible labour markets' and 'globalisation', New Travellers and Gypsies would appear to represent the ultimate flexible labour squad, or what the sociologist Anthony Giddens has recently termed 'portfolio workers'. They travel where the work is and can adapt to changed circumstances very quickly.

New Travellers and Gypsy status

It is not always clear whether New Travellers are to be classed as Gypsies for the purposes of the 1960 Caravan Sites Act. That is to say, do local authorities have the power under this Act to provide them with sites? And can New Travellers claim any special consideration if they apply to open a private site as a base?

The operative wording in the Act is 'of nomadic habit of life' and the first question always asked is how long someone has to have been on the road to be so defined. In 1986 a Yorkshire court ruled that a group known as 'The Mutants' were Gypsies within the meaning of the Act. On the other hand a court in Berkshire ruled that a Ms B. had not proved 'her intent to be a Gypsy'.

The recent decision on appeal in the case of South Hams District Council v. Gibb (1994) has ruled that 'nomadism' means travelling with an economic purpose. This is further discussed below. Romany Gypsies living on a caravan site who travel only to visit fairs, to see friends and relatives, lose their status as 'Gypsies' under the 1960 Act. On the other hand, New Travellers who travel from a roadside camp either to work or to seek work may acquire the status of 'Gypsies'.

Self-representation: Friends, Families and Travellers Support Group

Steve Staines is a former soil scientist who re-trained as a teacher. He established Friends, Families and Travellers Support Group (FFT), which was based in Glastonbury, in the early 1990s as he was personally concerned for the future of some members of his family who were living on the road, his son and grand-daughter in particular. FFT appreciates that the nomadic way of life has much to offer but that, in a post-Criminal Justice Act Britain, the lifestyle is under threat. Since its humble beginnings, FFT has grown to be, unarguably, one of the best known support and campaigning groups around for New Travellers. Its networking principles and the enthusiasm of those who staff the group have ensured its growth and development around the country. The work of FFT has many dimensions, although attending and overseeing evictions, arranging planning appeals and organising conferences to help inform local authority and district council policy-makers are amongst some of its most important tasks. A network of FFT offices now exist up and down the country with the aim of providing advice and information for and about New Travellers. The main office of FFT is now located in Brighton and Susan (Alex) Alexander is one of the main co-ordinators.

7

Private Sites

Background

Because of the importance of private caravan sites for Gypsies at the present time, we devote a separate chapter to this issue in this new work. We must remember, though, that not all Gypsies can afford to buy land for a private site and that for those who need to travel throughout the year because of the nature of their work, private sites are not the solution. They need transit sites.

After the end of the Second World War in 1945 a number of Gypsies bought plots of land mainly to use as a winter base. However, a Caravan Sites Act in 1960 was followed by three Town and Country Planning Acts which made it almost impossible for individual Gypsies any longer to get planning permission to site their own caravan or for larger landowners, Gypsy or Gorgio, to build caravan sites.

Sites opened after 1960 without planning permission were closed by enforcement orders:

- In 1970 Dorking closed the site at the Journey's End Cafe.
- Sevenoaks required the 'discontinuance' of the Three Ways site.
- The then Hollingbourn Rural District Council used the 1962 Planning Act against two families on a caravan site called Leytonstone.

Hundreds of families were turned off their own land or other privately owned sites which did not have planning permission. Sites bought before 1960 which do not need planning permission because they had 'established use' have been refused site licences or they were taken over by councils and closed using Compulsory Purchase Orders:

- Greenbanks in Walton-on-Thames housed ninety caravans, mainly Gypsies. After the land had been purchased, the Council built houses on it, while the Gypsies were driven out of the area, as far as London.
- In 1971 Epsom took over Cox's Lane site, ran it for a while, and then turned the residents off. Some years later they had to reopen it as an official Gypsy site and let many of the original inhabitants on again. The unfortunate families from Cox's Lane had spent many years on the roadside because of this act of bureaucratic folly.

Local authorities just did not like the idea of large numbers of Gypsy families living freely in their area:

- Runnymede Council in 1987 evicted fifteen families including twenty-seven children from their own land in Egham. The Gypsies were offered accommodation in a bed and breakfast hotel at Basingstoke, some thirty miles away.
- The picturesque Greenwich site was taken over by the Council, its leafy alleyways removed, and a concrete field built, a design which won an architectural prize.
- Sevenoaks Council recently bought the private site at Swan Farm by compulsory purchase at agricultural value. They then gave themselves permission to change the use of the land to residential, built a caravan site and offered to sell the land back to the previous owners at a higher price than they had paid for it. Alternatively, the Gypsies could rent what had been their own land from the Council. Some families with children were not offered places on the new site and had to move.

Whenever a Council took over a site it reduced the number of families provided for and these too went to join the thousands on the road. The majority of the Romany Gypsies on the roadside at the time of the 1962 survey had been evicted from private sites.

Enforcement action against these privately owned sites had been condemned by central government in the now cancelled circular MHLG 38/70:

> Where local authorities are considering the timing of planning enforce-
> ment action against travelling families who may have bought a plot of
> land and have stationed their caravan on it without the necessary plan-
> ning permission and site licence, in some circumstances it may be possi-
> ble to defer enforcement action until sites have been established in the
> county to which such families could go.

In spite of this, local councils still issued enforcement orders. One
example from many was Chelmsford Council's action against Mr and
Mrs M. in 1988. Even though there were no sites in the district they
tried to force this family off their own land, justifying their action by the
danger of 'ribbon development' along the road.

A Mr Price let his elderly father stop in a caravan next to his bungalow in Leicestershire. Because the father cooked some of his own meals
and used an outside toilet rather than the toilet in the house, planning
permission was needed. Had he used the facilities in the bungalow,
siting his caravan next to it would have been legal. Because of this fine
point, the district council took enforcement action and Mr Price's father
had to leave the land.

The planning process

The first step in the process is to make an application to the local council
to change the previous use of the land (often grazing) to residential. In
some councils a committee of councillors makes the decision, in others
the task is delegated to officers in the planning department. At this stage
90 per cent of applicants are refused. Rejection in the Green Belt is
almost automatic.

In 1977 the Government, following the Cripps Report, asked for a
more sympathetic attitude in looking at planning applications, in
another withdrawn circular (DE 28/77):

> In view of the urgent need for more sites, local authorities may wish to
> consider the advantages of encouraging (Gypsy owned sites). It may
> involve a sympathetic and flexible approach to applications for planning
> permission and site licences.

This too was ignored. Only 10 per cent of applications were passed and
the rest were dropped or had to go to appeal. Thus in December 1987

Mr T. was refused permission by Epping Forest District Council, who stated:

> The proposal is contrary to Policy 36 of the Draft Local Plan which states that Planning Permission will not be granted for use of land as a Gypsy caravan site within the Local Plan Area.

A reason for rejection can always be found, for example:

> The proposed development is contrary to the provisions of Policy CS19 of the Mid Bedfordshire Local Plan, for the following reasons.
>
> (i) The visual appearance and nature of the development would be detrimental to the character and appearance of this part of Houghton Conquest.
>
> The site lies within an area where residential development would not normally be permitted. (Ashford Borough Council).

An appeal can be made against such a refusal and will eventually be considered by an Inspector appointed by the Planning Inspectorate in Bristol. It has been argued before the European Court that because the Inspectors work for the Government they are not neutral but the Court decided that, because, in some cases, there is the right of appeal to the normal courts, which are independent, the system is fair. But since such an appeal to the British courts was only possible on a point of law the European Court left it open for the decision to be tested in other cases where the basis for the appeal is on factual grounds rather than legal.

There is a higher rate of success with appeals than for initial applications although Gypsy sites are between two and three times more likely to be refused than other developments.

On appeal Gypsies often face a Catch 22 situation. Although they are supposed to be given special consideration, it has been argued by councils that the applicants, because they have bought land, are no longer of nomadic habit of life, so no longer Gypsies and, therefore, do not merit special consideration. This argument was accepted by a Department of the Environment Inspector in 1975:

> Turning to the submission that your client is a Gypsy who wishes a permanent home for himself, his wife and six children and should accordingly be treated as a special case, it was indicated to me that Mr Frankham's real desire was to build a bungalow on the appeal site and the

proposed caravan developments before me under appeal were somewhat inadequate alternatives. While this motive is commendable it appears to indicate, when coupled with the fact that Mr Frankham and his family have lived on the appeal site for five years, that he has given up his nomadic habit of life. I accordingly see no reason to disagree with the Magistrates' Court decision in 1972 that Mr Frankham was not a Gypsy in terms of Section 16 of the Caravan Sites Act.

Forced off his own land by this decision, Mr Frankham then had to wander the country before he again became legally a Gypsy.

Although in one similar case recently the Secretary of State overturned an Inspector's decision that a Gypsy who had settled down was no longer a Gypsy as defined by the 1968 Act, this view has not always been shared by the courts. Even if they are accepted as Gypsies they may not always benefit if the Inspector is unaware of or ignores Government policy. In Essex in 1980, in spite of earlier circulars, Mr A. the Inspector was 'not aware that Gypsies should be treated differently from other applicants.'

The Friends, Families and Travellers Support Group studied planning appeal decision letters for Gypsies and New Travellers from 1994 to 1997. They found that the success rate was 34 per cent of which only half were permanent permissions. Somewhat surprisingly there were more refusals for proposals in landscapes of local significance (such as Areas of Great Landscape Value) than those of national importance (for example, Areas of Outstanding Natural Beauty).

A previously mentioned survey, *Private Gypsy Site Provision* by Toby Williams, examining the results of applications at the first level was published by ACERT in September 1999.

Private sites and planning law

The stationing of caravans requires permission under the Town and Country Planning Act of 1990. Circular 1/94 makes it difficult to get permission in protected areas. There are many of these ranging from Green Belts and National Parks, through Areas of Outstanding Natural Beauty, Special Landscape Areas, Areas of Special Landscape Value, Coastal Conservation Areas, not to mention Strategic Gaps and Green Wedges. The Lea Valley Park covering hundreds of acres has resisted all attempts to establish Gypsy sites whether by local authorities or private owners.

In all, probably over 50 per cent of the country is covered by such designations and if we add the built-up area it leaves very few places where Gypsies can get planning permission for a private site.

Because of Circular 1/94 and another Government document known as PPG2, to get permission to station a caravan in the Green Belt needs 'very special circumstances' – the term used in PPG2. In the case of a Special Landscape Area or Area of Outstanding Natural Beauty it has been argued that only 'special circumstances' are required not 'very special circumstances'.

We now turn to see what happens on appeal. If the local authority refuses a planning application, an appeal can be made to the Planning Inspectorate as stated above. In the two years following the issue of circular 1/94 and the withdrawal of previous advice, the number of cases granted on appeal was low compared with most previous years. In 1994 26 per cent of appeals were allowed and in 1995 25 per cent. In 1985 on the other hand 56 per cent of cases which went to appeal were passed.

The survey by Friends, Families and Travellers Support Group looked at appeal decision letters from 1994 to 1997. On the basis of incomplete figures for 1996 and 1997 the analysis suggests a rise in successes during those years although not reaching the level of earlier periods. The survey notes that half of the positive appeal decisions were for temporary permissions with an average of less than three years being granted. These were normally allowed on the grounds of a personal need rather than the lack of Gypsy sites as such.

Many planning consultants feel that decisions are irrational. A site which is passed in one area by one Inspector might be refused elsewhere by another. A typical refusal letter concludes:

> The site is very open and exposed to direct views from the adjoining roads. In my opinion, the caravans, associated structures and domestic paraphernalia represent an alien development ... in this rural area.

On the other hand, a site outside the village of Queen Charlton in the Bristol Green Belt was passed for three years. The Inspector said:

Gypsies on this private site in Hertfordshire are mostly small businessmen need-
ing no support from the State; *photograph by Bill Forster*

> In this case I consider that at this moment the combination of the
> acknowledged local need for Gypsy sites, the absence of any local provi-
> sion … the absence of serious harm to the interests of landscape and the
> amenity of occupiers of nearby land and buildings and the important
> material consideration of Mr O'Connor's agreed Gypsy status amount to
> very special circumstances which outweigh the strong policy presump-
> tion against this inappropriate development in the Green Belt.

A number of Gypsies have bought a bungalow with the intention of the
older members of the family living inside while the younger ones live in
caravans in the grounds. The rules allowing this as 'lawful development'
are very strict. The caravan has to be within the curtilage of the house
and the occupants have to use its facilities (such as the kitchen). As a Mr
Boswell found out to his cost, the existence of an outside toilet was also
to disqualify his disabled brother from living in a caravan at the side of
the residence. It is possible to apply for planning permission but this is

rarely, if ever granted. Mr Boswell's application is currently under appeal.

New hurdles

Councils have also used the need for a site licence to stop the development of a site which has received planning permission. This is done by imposing conditions which cannot be met such as the provision of mains electricity and water services. This is still being done in spite of the decision of Mr Widdicombe QC in the High Court in the case of Stirrup v. Secretary of State for the Environment and Carrick District Council in 1993. He ruled that the model standards issued by the Government do not apply to Gypsy sites.

Every planning application asks for details of how surface water is to be disposed of. For years it has been sufficient to write 'soakaway' – if you place a caravan in a field (possibly on a hard standing) any rain seeps away through the ground. Suddenly the Environment Agency is demanding a certificate of permeability – an extra chore and expense for the Gypsy who is trying to find somewhere to pull off from the road.

South Gloucestershire wrote to a Gypsy who had just obtained planning permission asking for 'full details on the construction, type and location of the soakaway system, including any connection points for carriageways, footpaths, paved areas, as well as buildings and any discharge points for the drainage system'.

The same letter also stated that a site licence would not be issued if there was only a stand-alone portaloo.

Inspectors at work

Refusal of planning permission by Government appointed Inspectors can mean that a family has lost its life savings purchasing land that is now worthless and also have to go back on the road, taking children out of school. Some of the refusals are hard to understand.

Case One

Mr and Mrs Smith bought a piece of land on the edge of the village of Houghton Conquest that had been used as a builder's yard. They moved there with their two grown-up children and one grandchild. Planning permission was refused.

Even though the government circular 1/94 recommends sites on the outskirts of built-up areas as being suitable, the Inspector ruled against the site because it was outside the village envelope.

Then it was ruled that Mr and Mrs Smith were no longer Gypsies. This was because Mrs Smith had signed an affidavit when she first applied for permission from the district council saying she wanted to settle down. This was used as evidence that she was no longer a Gypsy. Her husband was also denied Gypsy status because his travels were mainly as a preacher at religious conventions.

So the family must leave the site and travel again. Mr and Mrs Smith will be re-established as statutory Gypsies but they will have lost their site.

Case Two

Mr W. married a non-Gypsy and for a time lived on his father's caravan site but relationships between his wife and his parents deteriorated and so he bought a piece of land a few hundred metres away and moved on. There was a large barn on the land which hid the caravan from view by cars on the main road. After he had bought the land, the area was designated as an area of local landscape importance.

The Inspector refused planning permission because of this and said the couple should go back to Mr W's father's land. A second Inspector reversed this decision but the Council appealed to the High Court and it was only after a costly hearing that the W's finally won the right to stay on their own land.

Case Three

Another Inspector was responsible for turning some twenty Gypsy and New Traveller families off land belonging to a friendly farmer, one of the few who is willing to have Gypsies and Travellers on his land. The reasons for the refusal included:

The relative lack of public transport which is available does not fall within in my definition of there being a reasonable access to facilities.

One criterion in Policy G2 of the CSP is that the site should be of a size which enables the residents to be assimilated within the local community. Therefore because Upper Hill only consists of thirtyt-two house-holds I consider that the addition of a further twenty-six or thirty house-holds of Gypsies or Travellers would not enable assimilation into the local community to take place.

With all these obstacles, the reader may wonder whether anyone ever does get permission. The figures show that between 1989 and 1998 a total of 1,800 additional private pitches were provided on some 900 sites – an average of one site being approved per week. This has to be judged against the figures cited above, that 90 per cent of applications are refused by local councils. About half of these have then gone forward to appeal, at which stage between a third and a half are rejected. Both these figures are higher than for planning applications as a whole. Against the successful 900 Gypsies who have obtained planning permission (for an average of two caravans each) must be placed the 3,600 unsuccessful applications, at a cost of over £500,000 for the fees to the local authority alone.

Lord Avebury (who, as Erick Lubbock was responsible for piloting the 1968 Caravan Sites Act through the House of Commons) has

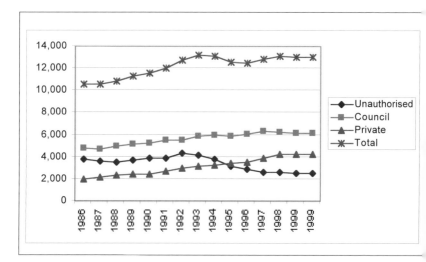

Pitches on private sites, council sites and unauthorised sites (1986-99)

written to Nick Raynsford, a minister at the Department of the Environment, Transport and the Regions (DETR) pointing out that local authority accommodation is declining and that provision of private sites is levelling out. Lord Avebury has kindly provided the graph on the previous page.

Enforcement

What happens if a Gypsy is refused planning permission for a private site?

If a local council refuses planning permission for a private site it will normally then issue an enforcement notice ordering the residents to quit the site within perhaps six months and to remove any fences and hard-standing. It is possible to appeal against such an enforcement order just as one can appeal against the refusal of planning permission.

If there is no appeal or if the enforcement order is upheld by the Government-appointed Inspector, the local council will then take steps to remove the family. Circular 1/94 which purports to help Gypsies get private sites gives very clear instructions to councils on how to evict Gypsies from their own land if they do not have planning permission.

Without entering into the complexities of the law, councils have three options:

1. They can take the residents to court for breach of planning law for which fines of up to £20,000 can and have been imposed. These fines are considerably higher than those for trespassing on someone else's property.
2. They can ask a judge to issue an injunction ordering the family to leave. This means the Gypsies could be imprisoned for contempt of court if they do not do so.
3. Thirdly, they can come along with a bull-dozer and push the caravans on to the road. Maidstone has taken this action at least twice.

In 1993 Guildford Council tried to get some caravan dwellers imprisoned because they had not left the land after an injunction had been granted. Judge Sedley, however, ruled that there was no evidence that they had deliberately disobeyed the order and they could only be fined, not imprisoned.

A Gypsy in Sussex who, on principle, refused to pay a fine for staying on his land without permission was sentenced to prison and ended up sharing a cell with a murderer.

Taking the Gypsies to court for a breach of planning law gives some possible chance for staying on the site. The lawyer for William Thomas of Basildon argued that there was no way he could comply with a notice to leave his land as there were no legal alternatives possible. The jury returned a verdict of not guilty.

He was more fortunate than Mr Beard who was heard in the Court of Appeal where there is no jury. The judges ruled that no such defence could be pleaded. However, a loophole remains, and this relies on a point made by Lord Justice Bingham in 1997 when he said: 'When a suitable case arises the correctness of [the judgement in] Regina v. Beard should be considered by the House of Lords'.

It seems, however, at present, that it is not sufficient defence to show there is no alternative to staying on your own land without permission except trespassing on someone else's land. It is possible that if a Gypsy has some relatives living on his land and is served with an injunction to remove them, he could not be expected to do so by force. This needs to be tested in a higher court.

Who is a Gypsy? – (1)

Although for the purposes of the 1976 Race Relations Act Gypsies are an ethnic group, for the 1960 Caravan Sites Act and planning purposes they were a social group, 'persons of nomadic habit of life'. Lord Bridge, in the case of Greenwich LBC v. Powell (House of Lords November/December 1988), suggested in an aside that seasonal nomadism was necessary to retain a nomadic habit of life and Gypsy status. (It was being argued that some of the tenants on the Greenwich Gypsy site were not Gypsies as they travelled only in the summer).

This guidance was followed by the High Court in a case involving an appeal against the refusal of planning permission – Horsham DC v. Secretary of State for the Environment and Mark Giles (13 October 1989). The High Court overruled the decision of an inspector that Mr Giles *was* a Gypsy and said that, although he was of Romany origin, he no longer had Gypsy status because he had stopped travelling. He was not, therefore, entitled to special consideration in his planning application for a private site.

Lord Bridge's remarks were refined by the further ruling in the case of South Hams v. Gibb (1994). The judges said that not only must there be at least seasonal nomadism, but this nomadism must be for an economic purpose. Wandering aimlessly around the countryside is not nomadism.

Maidstone Council queried the Gypsy status of a Mr Dunn. The High Court ruled that he was a Gypsy as 'the amount of nomadism does not have to be substantial'.

At many enquiries where Gypsies are trying to get permission to station a caravan on their own land much time is spent debating whether the applicant has lost his Gypsy status. It comes as a surprise to the applicant that, even though all his life he has been treated as a Gypsy both by his family and the local pub, he is no longer one when it comes to trying to get sympathetic consideration for trying to find a place to legally stop.

More information on this subject is given in the following section.

Who is a Gypsy? – (2)

This section deals in more detail with the definition of 'Gypsy' in Planning Law.

Even after Department of the Environment circular 1/94 (see pages 106 and 147) the fact that an applicant for planning permission is a Gypsy is a material factor and therefore it is important to define who is and who is not a 'Gypsy' in British law.

Etymologically the word 'Gypsy' comes from Egyptian and logically should therefore be spelled with a capital letter. It was the name given to the Romanies when they came to western Europe as it was thought that they came from Egypt. In fact, it is generally accepted that they came from India.

Until 1967 it was considered that the word Egyptian/Gypsy applied to a race, and indeed a foreign race. Thus, Henry VIII in 1530 imposed a ban on the immigration of 'Egipcions' and notice was given to all Egipcions in England to leave the country.

In 1554, Mary Tudor's government reaffirmed this. Egyptians were forbidden to enter the country and provisions made for the capital punishment of Egyptians if they remained in the country for more than one month.

In 1783, all existing laws concerning Gypsies were repealed. However, in 1822 the Turnpike Roads Act and in 1835 the Highway Act re-introduced the term 'Gypsy' into legislation. The Highway Act of 1835 (5 and 6 William IV c.50 s.72,76) penalised Gypsies who camped on the highway to a fine of 40 shillings. The later Highways Act of 1959 § 127 said:

> If … Gypsy pitches a booth, stall or stand, or encamps on a highway he shall be guilty of an offence …

For over a hundred years Gypsies camped on the highway regularly and paid up their 40 shillings until 1967 when a Mr Cooper contested a case and pleaded not guilty, saying he was not a Gypsy, as it could not be proved that he was descended from Indian immigrants and of Romany race.

At this point it became necessary for the courts to decide on the definition of the term 'Gypsy'. The Divisional Court in 1967 finally laid down that – as British law could not nowadays be discriminating against a race – the definition of Gypsy for the purposes of the Highways Act must refer to a way of life.

Lord Parker said:

> I think that in this context 'Gypsy' means no more than a person leading a nomadic life with no, or no fixed, employment and with no fixed abode.

Lord Diplock indicated his view that 'Gypsy' in the section bore:

> its popular meaning, which I would define as a person without a fixed abode who leads a nomadic life dwelling in tents or other shelters or in caravans or other vehicles (Mills v. Cooper 1967)

The 1968 Caravan Sites Act did not adopt this definition of Gypsy but gave a wider definition.

> Persons of nomadic habit of life, whatever their race or origin.

It seems clear that the person who drafted the Act was aware that they were not following the earlier 1967 definition.

The next relevant case was Greenwich v. Powell (1988) which defined a 'Gypsy' caravan site in reference to the position of Gypsy sites as opposed to other caravan sites. As previously stated, the Caravan Sites Act of 1968 and a later Mobile Homes Act made a distinction between Gypsy caravan sites run by councils and other sites. In particular, tenants of pitches on Gypsy sites have no rights.

The question before the court was whether the Greenwich Gypsy site was a Gypsy site for the purposes of the acts. The Lords decided that if the Council had set up a Gypsy site it did not matter whether the people on it were Gypsies or not, the site remained a Gypsy site for legal purposes.

During the course of making their decision there was an obiter (as an aside) definition of a Gypsy. Lord Bridge said:

> I am inclined to conclude … that a person may be within the definition if he leads a nomadic life only seasonally and notwithstanding that he regularly returns for part of the year to the same place where he may be said to have a fixed abode or residence.

This means that a person can be settled for part of the year but as long as they travel they are still legally Gypsies.

This was also important at that time because the Caravan Sites Act made a distinction between Gypsies and non-Gypsies stopping in areas designated under the Act and also because of circulars from the Ministry of Housing and Department of the Environment in which councils were encouraged to give planning permission to Gypsies.

With the emergence from the late 1960s and early 1970s of New Travellers (see chapter 6) the question arose as to whether non-Romanies could be classed as Gypsies if they were nomadic.

The key case is that of Mrs Capstick and others (in 1986). Judge Herrod held that:

> [The] defendants had adopted, and intended to continue with, a travelling life-style and [travelled] basically from Yorkshire to the West Country and back during the year. None of the defendants, with one possible exception, came from families with a tradition of travelling but they had adopted such a life for various reasons e.g. force of circumstances, the absence of settled accommodation and attraction to the way of life.

He held that 'the applicants were Gypsies within the meaning of the

Caravan Sites Act of 1968 as they were on the evidence 'persons of nomadic habits of life.'

The definition (of nomadic habit of life) was later refined in the case of Regina v. S. Hams ex parte Gibb 1994 referred to above. It was established by this case that to be a Gypsy one had to travel for an economic purpose:

> The definition of 'Gypsies' in section 16 (of the 1968 Act) imported the requirement that there should be some recognisable connection between the wandering or travelling and the means whereby the persons concerned made or sought their livelihood.

This judgement was clouded by the statements of two of the judges that to be a Gypsy one had to travel in a group. Travelling in groups is now difficult as the 1994 Criminal Justice and Public Order Act for practical purposes stops Gypsies travelling in groups as if more than two families (two lorries and two caravans) stop in one place, they will have more than five vehicles and will be committing aggravated trespass under the Act. If we took together Lords Neil and Millett's opinion that to be a Gypsy one must travel in a group and the Act which forbids caravanners to travel in groups, this would mean that there are no more Gypsies.

Lord Justice Leggatt, the third judge in the case, however, said:

> The term (Gypsy) was not expressly confined to those who travelled in groups and the Act did not stipulate that persons could not be Gypsies unless they did so.

Finally, the case of Dunn v. Maidstone and the Secretary of State (1996) had established the principle that the total amount of money earned during the period he travelled does not have to be more than the amount earned while not travelling. Maidstone had contested the Inspector's opinion that Mr Dunn was a Gypsy. However, the Court found as follows:

> (Mr Dunn's) main occupation and source of income is from landscape gardening around the Maidstone area which does not normally entail other than daily travel to work. However, I note that he also breeds horses of which he currently owns eight and travels to horse fairs including Appleby, Stow-on-the-Wold and the New Forest where he buys and sells horses... He could be away for up to two months of the year at least partly in connection with a traditional Gypsy activity which I consider ...

> also has an economic justification. I do not therefore conclude that taking
> into account the relatively short time during which he has adopted a gen-
> erally more settled lifestyle, the appellant has so abandoned travelling as
> to lose his status as a Gypsy under s.16 of the 1968 Act.

The importance of these cases is that they mean a Gypsy family can settle during the winter and let their children go to school while travelling
mainly in the Easter and summer holidays for an economic purpose and
retaining Gypsy status.

It is possible for house-dwellers to obtain Gypsy status if they start to
travel, and the question arises – how long do you have to travel to
become a statutory (legal) Gypsy? The now defunct Avon Council established the principle in their area that New Travellers had to travel for at
least two years before the Council would class them as Gypsies.

If someone is brought up as a Gypsy how long can they be settled
without losing Gypsy status? An early case where it was ruled that an
ethnic Romany was not a statutory Gypsy is Horsham DC v. Secretary of
State and Giles (Queens Bench 1989) referred to above when Judge
McCullough said:

> Clearly there can, and indeed must, come a time when as a matter of fact
> the nomadic habit of life has been lost. When it is lost the Gypsy is no
> longer a Gypsy for the purposes of the Act.

Mr Giles had lived at Billinghurst on the same site continuously since
1969 and before then in another settled place in Worthing since 1957 –
a total of thirty-two years, by far the majority of his life. It was argued on
Mr Giles' behalf that he was part of a family group, some members of
which had travelled a great deal, and therefore, he was of nomadic habit
of life, but this was not accepted by the judge.

This judgement was reaffirmed in Cuss v. Secretary of State and
Wychavon when Judge Vandermeer said:

> [it is] clear that the element of the nomadic habit of life had to be present
> albeit that it might be seasonal.

The Inspector had found that 'the predominant picture was of a relatively settled life-style' and that Mr Cuss did not appear to have undertaken
any regular seasonal migration or other travelling apart from occasional
moves in search of a permanent pitch. However, the case note reminds us

that [Gypsy] status can be regained again and so if the Cuss family were to take up again even just seasonal travelling the status could be regained.

Periods from two to five years have been suggested as the length of time spent without nomadising after which Gypsy status would be lost. It is also suggested that New Travellers would lose their status more quickly (and regain it more slowly) than an ethnic Gypsy. In the case of a Mr Stacey – also in 1990 – it was ruled he was not a Gypsy because he had a mobile home (not a touring caravan) and lived on a private site not a council Gypsy site.

A further question arises – is it ever possible to stop travelling but retain Gypsy status? The answer is yes, in certain circumstances. In the case of illness of the person or a relative, Gypsy status is retained while not travelling as long as there is an intention to resume travel at some time. (This was decided in R. v. Shropshire CC ex parte Bungay 1990).

If Gypsies stop travelling because of old age they retain their status. This was agreed by the Inspector in a planning case (Mr Luderman) although there is no higher level authority for this belief.

It was discussed informally in the planning case of a Mr P. whether, if a Gypsy is prevented from travelling because of a prison sentence, is he still a Gypsy? The Council felt that he should not benefit from being allowed to keep his Gypsy status because he had committed a crime. However, the punishment for committing the crime was a prison sentence. It would be unfair if, in addition to a prison sentence, the Gypsy also lost his status and the right to live on his own land. In the event, the planning appeal was refused on another ground, the Inspector was not told why Mr P. was not present and no decision was taken on whether Mr P was still a Gypsy.

Logically, the act of applying for permission to reside on land implies the intention to give up travelling and therefore cease to be a Gypsy. The applicant would be refused permission on the grounds that he was not a Gypsy. He would therefore have to go back on the road and become a Gypsy again. However, there seems to be no logical reason why applying for a bungalow should mean loss of Gypsy status (as was ruled in the case of Mr Frankham above). Living in a bungalow for the rest of the year when not travelling seems no different from living on a fixed pitch on a caravan site. Indeed, some families have many problems obtaining insurance on their caravans, through no fault of their own, and therefore have no option but to move into a bungalow. In the study by Barbara Adams and others, they included families whom they found travelling in the summer although they had a house in the winter.

In the case of a man who was brought up as a Gypsy and who married a house-dweller, we may arrive at the situation where the husband has Gypsy status but the wife has not yet gained this status. If planning permission is given for Gypsies, not as a personal permission for Mr X and his immediate family, then theoretically the wife would not be allowed to live on the site.

Any children born during a period of settlement would not have Gypsy status and also would be unable to live on the site. This may be an argument for Inspectors to make permissions personal prior to some resolution of this apparent paradox.

Inspectors have wondered how long each year does a person have to travel to retain Gypsy status? The comment in Notes of Cases on Dunn (see above) says: 'This sporadic nomadic life ...does not have to be very substantial.' Mr Dunn travelled for 'up to two months each year.'

In the case of the Greenwich site the occupants (at the time of the case) were allowed to leave the site for twenty weeks, paying half rent, without losing their pitch.

References have been made by Inspectors and judges to 'traditional occupations'(e.g. a reference to 'a traditional Gypsy activity' as we have seen in the Dunn case). However, Gypsies' occupations are not static and have changed over the years adapting to new markets. For example, a Mr Fuller was refused Gypsy status because he sold farm equipment and this was not considered to be a traditional Gypsy occupation.

When Romanies first came to Europe some were snake charmers and acrobats. In the early part of this century, common occupations were door-to-door selling of clothes pegs and crochet work, fortune telling and for the men – casual farm work. Times have changed and tarmac'ing, roofing and garden landscaping are important new ways of earning a living. In the case of New Travellers with Gypsy status, occupations have included running a vegetarian canteen at fairs. There seems no reason for the economic activity practised to be a traditional Gypsy trade.

8

Gypsies and majority society

Discrimination

Romanies and Irish Travellers have suffered discrimination by being refused service in public houses and shops, entry to dance halls and youth clubs, even on at least one occasion (in Sheffield) not allowed on a bus.

Discrimination is not a new phenomenon. Here is an example taken from an article in *The Countryman* recalling the 1920s:

> In season, the itinerants poured in, to pea pick, single out and so on; tramps, Gypsies and Travellers of every kind. 'No Gypos' read the notice on the pub door.

The Commission for Racial Equality and its predecessor, the Race Relations Board, received many complaints in particular about pubs with 'No Gypsies' signs outside. Letters 'achieved some success' in the removal of signs but recently new wording 'No Travellers' has been used. Under the Race Relations Act such a sign may be seen as discriminating *indirectly* against Romany Gypsies. The pub owner would need to justify the sign and a suitable test case is awaited to see how these notices could be justified. Under the Race Relations Act only the CRE can prosecute a discriminator. All that Gypsies can do is refer these signs, and refusals of service, to the CRE and leave it to the Commission to decide which cases to take up.

Notices are becoming more subtle, such as 'Travellers by Appointment only', so that a Gypsy with limited reading ability will see the sign as applying to him, but in case of prosecution the landlord

This popular riverside pub in Hertfordshire displays a 'No Travellers' sign; *photographs by Bill Forster*

might get away with arguing that he was referring to commercial travellers. It has been reported to the Internet Traveller discussion list that a number of public houses in west London are painting white crosses on their door as a sign to Gypsies that they will not be welcome.

In two cases where clubs rather than pubs were concerned, the cases were settled out of court with an apology to the Traveller who had been refused entry. One involved an Irish Traveller but, because it never reached the stage of a trial, the argument that Irish Travellers are an ethnic group has never been settled in a British court.

One of the few cases where Race Relations legislation was pursued to a conclusion was in the village of Brymbo in Wales.

Gypsy family J. lived in a caravan in a gravel pit in this village. Both parents had been born in nearby villages and had lived in the area all their lives. They had ten children. In 1978 they registered on the housing waiting list and in 1980 a house became vacant and it was expected that it would be offered to the family.

A local house dweller Mrs S. organised a petition headed: 'We the

signatories of the attached petition wish to state that we object strongly
to the housing of a further Gypsy family in Brymbo'. Over 300 local
residents signed the petition. Mrs S. was reported in a local paper as saying that there was already one Gypsy family in the vicinity and that she
thought that the district where this empty house was situated was likely
to become 'a Gypsy site'. She was further reported as saying that 'the
Gypsies will move in here over our dead bodies'.

In May 1981, the CRE ruled that Mrs S., a Mrs G. and the Brymbo
Community Council had 'attempted to induce Wrexham and Maelor
Borough Council to discriminate unlawfully in the disposal of council
housing in contravention of the Race Relations Act'. They were ordered
to stop their campaign.

Discrimination in the field of employment has been widely reported.
Cases reported from Kent include a male Traveller who was turned
down for work as a night watchman when he gave as his address the
local caravan site. A young woman from the same site was also rejected
for factory work, with the added problem that because of her age (17)
she was also being refused Income Support.

A successful lottery award to an Aberdeen-based Travellers
Education project in early March 1999 caused an outcry in the local
area. The National Lottery Charities Board award of £175,000 was
granted to help improve conditions in the community for Travelling
People aged between twelve and twenty-five. It is also believed to be the
first of its type in the UK. A number of local residents are currently
objecting to the project and have dubbed it a 'waste of money'. David
Simmers, a founder member of the project, defended Travellers and said
they were being 'kept out' because they are different. He said:

> They are a group of people that are regularly discriminated against and
> excluded by society. People are often prejudiced and through ignorance
> they have a stereotypical view of them. It is our aim to identify and
> address the problems which Travellers face. For instance they often don't
> have access to education or other services....we want to encourage trav-
> ellers to act on their priority issues and generate a community identity for
> their own benefit.

However, Richard Cowling, a local businessman, attacked the charities
board for their 'infuriating and blatant waste of cash':

> I strongly object to charitable money being used for these types of
> schemes. I understand that travellers are a group of people who have their
> own culture but it is people like us that are usually left to clean up after
> them. Do they pay rates? No. Do they pay taxes? No. So why, when there
> are so many needy groups out there does this project get given so much
> money.

Kay Caldwell, of the National Lottery Charities Board, said the project
was chosen because it fitted the community involvement category.
However, to locals it was still a 'waste of money'.

Police – 'Gypsies are trouble'

The police attitude towards Gypsies is ambivalent. On the one hand
they may be friendly, especially in country districts where police are
recruited locally, with individuals whose families they will have known
since childhood. Nevertheless, they have to stand by 'to prevent a breach
of the peace', i.e. assist council officials or court bailiffs to evict Gypsies.
The police know, even if the council and magistrates do not, that when
they move them on the caravans will not disappear but turn up again
somewhere else and the whole process will have to start again. As one
policeman said to a meeting of teachers and other workers with Gypsies:

> Gypsies are trouble. If I move them on, I get you people or the local vicar
> complaining about persecution and harassment – if I don't move them
> on, then the people in the houses complain to my sergeant that I haven't
> done my duty.

In many areas a police force may have a Gypsy Liaison Officer or the
Community Liaison Officer is in regular contact with local Gypsy
spokesmen. But harassment is still common.

Gypsies on unofficial sites see a police car draw up at five in the
morning, hear the bang on the caravan window with a baton. Police
may confiscate the water churn 'for checking' although they rarely
nowadays find a cooking pot to tip into the fire (an action recounted by
many older Gypsies).

A common complaint is the over-reaction in the case of minor problems. In Peterborough in 1987 a house-dweller reported to the police
that he thought a young child from the neighbouring official caravan

site had stolen his son's bicycle. A busload of police turned up to arrest an eleven year old boy. In the event no charges were laid.

In 1988, 150 police came to Outwood, in Surrey, to 'look for two stolen cars'. They then took a great deal of property from the caravans. Later the same day a child threw a stone at a police car. Fifty police in riot gear then rushed on to the site and 'did it over'.

In the same month, police descended on a site in Sussex and arrested all the men, who were held for two months without bail. The worst incident perhaps has been in the county of Bedfordshire where police carried out a 'mock raid' with machine guns on a roadside camp as a demonstration for visiting continental officers.

In Sheffield there were a few officers whom the Gypsies nicknamed 'The Gypsy Squad':

> They drive on to the sites at two or three in the morning with blue lights flashing on their cars and just sit in their cars on the site. On one occasion they came with a warrant for a thirty year old man and because they couldn't find him they took away a seventeen year old on the same warrant.

On 7th October 1997 over 200 police raided an official site at Bloxham in north Oxfordshire, broke down the doors of caravans and prevented children from going to school. Residents said the officers swore and shouted insults including "Hitler had the right idea". They spent eleven hours on the site and found little to justify the raid.

A dispute between neighbours can lead to mass intervention. Armed police surrounded a Gypsy site in Cornwall in 1998 for more than five hours after a family feud. More than fifty police including a firearms unit moved in to seal off the camp. The dawn raid was carried out simultaneously with another raid as more than 100 police swooped on a second site in the area.

A five year- old Irish Traveller in 1998 was playing cowboys and Indians with a toy gun when ten armed police arrived wearing flak jackets and surrounded the caravans in a Strood car park. The police searched the caravans, As one mother said: 'They searched through all our cupboards, including my underwear'. Three hours later the police left the site empty handed.

Under the Criminal Evidence Act of 1985 police can arrest anyone and hold them for forty-eight hours. The magazine *City Limits* reported that under-age children were being held in police stations under this law. While researching the first edition of this pamphlet, the authors were told that Irish and English Travellers on unauthorised stopping places were being threatened with arrest under the Prevention of Terrorism Act unless they moved off.

Social Security

Traditionally, Gypsies did not ask the State for help at any stage of their lives. Born with an aunt acting as midwife, looking after their own disabled children, supporting relatives and friends when money was short, having a 'whip round' for cash to replace someone's burnt out caravan and supporting their aged parents in a bungalow. But times have changed. Families and friends can no longer stay together because of site regulations and the disappearance of the larger traditional stopping places. Craft work is hard to sell and in a country with several million unemployed there is less call for the odd job man, as the out-of-work and poor do their own repairs and gardening and keep their cars and refrigerators until they are too old for resale, even as scrap metal.

Farm labour has been replaced by machines or Gorgio women are bussed in from neighbouring towns. Daily horoscopes in the paper are cheaper than the palm reader. A breadwinner may have a spell in prison because of some vehicle or driving offence. Further, rules on official sites prevent any work being done near the caravan. Poverty exists in many sections of the Travelling community and Gypsies – for the first time – have to turn to social services for support and to the Benefits Agency for cash. But this is not easy:

> There seems to be an inconsistency of treatment towards the Travellers compared with anybody else claiming. A typical example (from Port Talbot) is that most people would be required to sign on once every two weeks in order to get benefit whereas with Travellers here the DHSS [as the Benefits Agency was then known] expects them to sign on every day. They won't give them travelling expenses for that and the only way to do it is to walk or take a cut in food money to pay for the bus.

And again from the same area:

> In some areas, DHSS offices will pay with one form of identification, whereas in this particular area you won't be paid without two. We had one case of a woman with five children who had to wait two or three weeks before she received any money from the DHSS. She survived on charity parcels from the Salvation Army and the Church Army.

Circular S50 issued in 1985, *Verification of Identity – Preventing Fraud*, caused problems for many Gypsies. This circular instructed DHSS offices not to accept baptismal certificates as a means of identity. They should ask for full birth certificates or driving licences. This particularly hit Irish Travellers whose births was often not registered and, of course, not all Gypsy women hold driving licences.

The North London Regional Fraud Office designed its own Itinerant Caravan Dwellers Information Card. It asked DHSS officers to record 'physical features, skin colour, known associates and criminal record'. This card was withdrawn after pressure from a Citizens Advice Bureau. However, in 1986 the DHSS convened the Nomadic Claimants Working Party intended mainly to deal with New Travellers. In 1986 this Working Party reported and suggested setting up a regional index. The form from which we print extracts below appears to be the one used for this index.

> Nomadic claimant
> The following claim has been made.
> 1. Name
> 6. Identity confirmed: Yes or No.
> If Yes, state means of identity accepted.
> 7. Description and other distinguishing features.
> Known by any other names (give details)

The form was to go to the Supplementary Benefit Section Regional Office in Gabalfa, Wales. Item 7 seems to imply that a nomadic claimant is likely to be simultaneously claiming at more than one office. Yet anyone with experience of a Benefits Agency office will know that claiming is a full-time job in itself in one place let alone two different offices (in spite of the occasional case that hits the headlines).

At the end of 1987, the S. family had all their documents taken away, suspected of being forgeries. While waiting for their return they had to move to another town where the local Travellers Support Group assisted them in obtaining duplicate birth and marriage certificates. Even today, not all Gypsies have either of these certificates. Many still just have a Romany wedding.

The Social Fund, which replaced Special Needs Payments, is unlikely to make payments, which are normally repayable loans, to any of the over 3,000 Gypsy families with no fixed address. Sixteen and seventeen-year olds are having difficulties in complying with rules for benefit, under which they have to get on a training course and find an employer who will take them as a trainee. This is difficult enough for a Gypsy on a caravan site and impossible for the nomad.

More recently, it has been the job of the Benefits Agency (BA) and the Employment Services (ES) to administer and deliver the payment of benefits to claimants. As part of the 'Thatcher revolution' in the public sector, new Public Management techniques were introduced and the Next Steps project led to the creation of a multitude of government executive agencies of which the BA was one. In effect, Next Steps saw a separation of policy from practice. The Department of Social Security (DSS) took overall lead on policy direction whilst the BA and ES took the lead on implementing policy and paying out benefits.

A study conducted by Action Group on Irish Youth (AGIY) in 1992-3 examined the experiences of Irish people, Travellers, the single homeless and ethnic minority groups when claiming benefits. AGIY was interested to see what kinds of identity checks were being made by the BA when new claims from these groups were being made. From the 'case studies' section of the report that deals with Travellers, it is clear that the social security system does treat Gypsies and other Travellers in a dis-criminatory manner. Of the eight cases documented, the experiences of 'Sean' were typical:

> Sean is a young Irish Traveller living in London for less than a year. He makes a claim for Income Support and provides an original copy of his birth certificate. The claim is automatically referred for further investigation to the Fraud Section. The claim is delayed pending investigation; on a number of previous occasions attempts by Sean to claim benefit have been similarly delayed. Sean said he felt he had so much difficulty because he is from a Traveller background.

Health

- The average life expectancy of a Gypsy is 48 years
- Only two out of every 100 Gypsies reach the age of 65
- Gypsy men die 10 years earlier than non-Gypsies on average
- Gypsy women die 12 years earlier than non-Gypsies on average
- Infant mortality rates for Travellers are some four times the national average.

It is clear from these stark figures (from a 1986 survey covering an admittedly limited target group) and a number of later reports that the travelling life today is not particularly healthy. As Dr Heller, a GP, and Beryl Peck, a Health Visitor, reported in Sheffield:

> The problems caused by poor sanitation, inadequate water supply and poverty, as well as the stress and fear that Gypsy families live under, cause a variety of problems we would be more familiar with in less developed countries.

The reports list a number of conditions directly attributable to the adverse conditions in which the Gypsies had lived their lives, mainly on illegal sites: uncorrected squints, unrecognised deafness, eczema, untreated cuts and burns, tetanus, bronchitis, etc.

It was in Sheffield too that a research worker from the London School of Hygiene found in 1981 that a high percentage of all pregnancies ended in perinatal death (before the child was one month old). The report quotes the example of Mrs C. who: 'had to leave hospital the day after her child was stillborn. Fear of eviction made her rush back to her caravan. What chance wound infection?'

A survey carried out in Kent in 1986 by Dr Vaile and Ms Pahl of the Health Services Research Unit in Canterbury found, for example, that 35 per cent of all families had no means of receiving post which, as the authors point out, means that letters from clinics or hospitals do not reach the people to whom they are sent. Infant mortality figures were again higher than national and regional averages. The survey found that the places where Gypsies lived were 'areas which would not normally be used for residential development, such as an old rubbish tip, a site adjoining a motorway, a sewage plant or a busy railway line'.

A recent study by Derek Hawes (see bibliography) and other reports reveal that the situation has not changed much over the years. One health visitor tells of three deaths of Travellers in their thirties in her area in one year that could have been prevented. In the first case, influenza turned into pneumonia because the family were reluctant to call a doctor. The second was a case of cervical cancer where no screening had taken place and the third the result of hepatitis C through lack of knowledge of health risks.

Many nomadic Gypsies – as well as New Travellers – find it difficult to get treatment from a GP, although under the Terms of Service of a General Medical Practitioner (Regulation 19) doctors who refuse to take a person on to their list must still provide 'immediate necessary treatment' for up to fourteen days. In one documented case, a doctor in Wiltshire refused to treat a Gypsy woman and her daughter. The mother needed a further supply of penicillin and the daughter a letter of referral to a hospital. Some Traveller families will journey hundreds of miles to return to a doctor's surgery where they have been well received in the past.

Most families prefer to go to a casualty department where they will normally be accepted for treatment without discrimination. However, some casualty departments have a rule which states that if you have had symptoms for more than forty-eight hours they will not see you and instead the rejected patients are given the telephone number of a helpline which explains how to register with a GP. Some experts think the new financial arrangements for medical practices which came into force in April 1990 will not help Gypsies to get treatment. For example, doctors may be reluctant to start a series of immunisation with a Gypsy child if they think that the family will move on before the full series is completed. This would make it harder for the practice to reach the necessary percentage of children with completed immunisations for payment to be made hence they will lose funds. So far there is no evidence of this happening on a wide scale.

The health visitor is perhaps the main instrument in ensuring that Gypsy children can get the care they need and there is now a national association through which these professionals can get mutual support and exchange information. The National Association also aims to act as a national voice to highlight the impact of legislation and local policies on the health and welfare of the Traveller and Gypsy communities.

This brightly painted 'Playbus' run by the East Herts Playbus Charity makes popular weekly visits to sites in Hertfordshire. There are similar services in some other counties; *photograph by Bill Forster*

Health workers say that until a national policy is implemented to support equal access to health services, the differences in effectiveness and appropriateness of health care provided throughout the United Kingdom for Travellers will vary enormously. Some of the new contracts for health visitors fail to recognise the additional work required in work with Travellers. Health providers have to monitor ethnic groups under Department of Health rules but Gypsies and Travellers are not monitored in this way (unlike the new practice in education). It has to be said, however, that as long as many Gypsies and Travellers are forced to live on sites with no water, refuse collection and no guarantee that they will be allowed to remain from one day to the next, their health will suffer.

Education

After the English Education Act of 1902 extended compulsory schooling to the whole population of England and Wales, there was a need to
regularise the position of Gypsies. This was done in the Children's Act
of 1908 by which children of nomadic parents were required to attend
for only 200 half-day sessions (instead of the normal 380). This provision was rarely enforced and few children attended school. Since most
local councils put their efforts into moving Gypsy families out of their
areas, there was little enthusiasm for organising education for them.

After the founding of the Gypsy Council in 1966 the first caravan
school in Britain was run by volunteers on an old aerodrome in the summer of the following year. Following this, a number of short-lived
Romano Drom (Romany Road) schools were started in England and
Wales. In 1967 too, the Ministry of Education published the Plowden
Report *Children and their primary Schools* which described Gypsy children
as probably the most severely deprived group in the country.

In 1968 the National Gypsy Education Council (NGEC) was set up
with a committee of Gypsy activists and educationalists. Lady Plowden
(chair of the committee which produced the report) was invited to head
this new body and the NGEC with its respectable image was able to gain
more grants from charitable funds than had the Gypsy Council's own
Education Trust. An independent voluntary project was set up in the
Midlands which continued till 1976. Superseding this initial provision,
although overlapping it for a brief period, the West Midlands Education
Service for Travelling Children was created by a consortium of eleven
local education authorities. Over the years, voluntary schemes were
gradually replaced by LEA provision.

In 1973 the Department of Education and Science, under its HMI
Short Course programme for teachers, ran the first official course on the
Education of Travelling Children, organised by Donald Buckland HMI.
Twenty- three teachers attended. This course was repeated every year
until 1976 when it was changed to a bi-annual event. Some of the courses drew over 250 participants. The HMI Short Course programme was
eventually phased out with the last course being held in Winchester in
1987.

In the same year as the first HMI Short Course, the NGEC split and there were then two national organisations, the NGEC and a new body known as The Advisory Council [earlier Committee] for the Education of Romany and Other Travellers (ACERT). Both these organisations were engaged in furthering the cause of Gypsy and Traveller education. The NGEC recently recognised its wider brief by changing its name to the Gypsy Council for Education, Culture, Welfare and Civil Rights.

In 1977, Croydons Education Committee caused a furore when it refused to admit a girl called Mary Delaney, a name made up for a test case, to its schools on the ground that she was on an illegal caravan site within the area of the authority. A similar action by the London Borough of Enfield led to joint protests by the NGEC and ACERT, together with a threat to take the Government to the European Courts. The Crown Court ruled in favour of Mary Delaney and the Government responded by inserting a clause into the 1980 Education Act aiming to block the loophole by which Croydon might legally have been able to exclude children from illegal sites from schools. Circular 1/81 of the Department of Education and Science, declared explicitly the right of Gypsy and Traveller children to attend school:

> The reference to children in the area of the authority means that each authority's duty extends to all children residing in their area, whether permanently or temporarily. The duty thus embraces in particular travelling children, including Gypsies.

A regulation made by The Department for Education and Employment in 1997 allows Travellers' children to be registered at more than one school at the same time in order to be legally registered at each school attended whilst nomadising, but at the same time, maintain a school place at a base school.

Regular attendance at the same school by Gypsy and Traveller children living in houses or on permanent caravan sites is, for obvious reasons, more feasible than for the children from the 3,000 or so families who are still travelling from one unauthorised site to another, on account of an insufficient supply of legal stopping places. This situation can have a damaging impact on both school access and attendance. A recent report from the north of England tells how police came to a school and removed four children from the classroom at the same time as the local authority officials were evicting the parents and their caravan

A Traveller Education support teacher carries out an initial assessment of a Traveller child on joining the local school; *photograph by Kate Stockdale, Hertfordshire Traveller Education Project*

A Traveller child joins in the Literacy Hour at her local school; *photograph by Kate Stockdale, Hertfordshire Traveller Education Project*

from a roadside site. An eviction in the London Borough of Enfield, led to the death of a six year -old boy during removal from an unauthorised site mentioned above. Had the family been on a legal site, the child might very well have been in school on the fateful day.

Most Gypsy and Traveller parents, in theory at least, welcome the chance of primary education for their children. However, as their children reach puberty and the subjects on offer seem less relevant to real life (life within their community and earning one's living), attitudes change. Research has shown that as the children get older, attendance drops off. Some parents, worried that their offspring will learn to take drugs, swear and hear about sex from young house-dwellers, encourage their older daughters to stay at home and their sons to go out with other male Gypsies to learn about work at first hand, rather than attend school. It is likely that, for some families, only the possibility of attending single sex schools and a curriculum more orientated to practical activities will encourage a greater attendance by 11-16 year-olds.

Until the 1980s, the role of central government in the development of policy for Gypsy and Traveller children's education, was only modest: the belief being that local education authorities were best placed to decide on policy and practice which matched local needs and circumstances. In 1983 Her Majesty's Inspectors published an HMI Discussion Paper entitled *The Education of Travellers' Children.* This provided some case histories of good educational practice. At this time LEAs could receive additional financial support for the education of Gypsy and Traveller children under the arrangements known as the 'No Area Pool'. This was a fund set up and financed by local authorities to support provision for pupils who did not belong to any one local authority area.

With the reform of local government finance in 1987/8, the 'No Area Pool' was ended. In its place the government introduced a new specific grant for the education of Travellers and Displaced Persons (Section 210 of the 1988 Education Reform Act). This was followed by Circulars 10/90 and 11/92, both of which encouraged LEAs to be active in making viable provision for the education of Gypsies and Traveller children. Circular 10/90 included a Part B which indicated a model of good practice. In 1996 the specific grant was amended within the Education Act of that year and become known as Section 488.

The impact of central funding has been significant. Over 400

The Citizen

Gloucestershire's largest selling newspaper

WEDNESDAY, MARCH 25, 1998

30p Vol 126 No. 234

TALKback *Would you let your child go to school with gipsies?*
PAGE 10

TALKback your views on the news

Would you object to gipsy children?

CLASSROOMS were left half-empty when parents withdrew children from lessons at Coney Hill Primary School in Gloucester after gipsies camped on the playing fields. Some of the travellers' children have been attending lessons and those parents who refused to join the boycott have labelled the protesters "hysterical". We asked people on the streets of **Gloucester** whether they felt parents were right to keep their children at home.

DAVID CARPENTER (55), of Brockworth: "I'm a grandparent, and I would have done the same. It's detrimental to the area if rubbish is left all over the place and there could be a health problem."

NATALIE WILLIAMS (19), of Kingsholm: "I would have just sent them to school. They are discriminating against their beliefs and culture. Everybody should have an education."

SALLY MORGAN, from Hempsted: "It's the kids I feel sorry for, because they don't get an education. They shouldn't be that bad at their age. They are very small and hopefully would be able to mix."

JEAN BUNCE (70), of Tredworth: "I quite agree the gipsy children should have an education, but if they are going to be disruptive, I can understand parents keeping their kids away. It's a difficult situation." Her husband Jarvis (67): "Maybe the gipsy children should get a special teacher."

JANE TWIGG, from Minsterworth: "There shouldn't be any discrimination just because they are travellers. They have a right to an education."

Have your say. Tonight's VoteLine question is: Would you send your child to school with travellers' children? **YES: 0891 112207 NO: 0891 112209**

Calls charged at 10p per minute. Lines are open noon to midnight

Would this question be asked about coloured children? The 'Talkback' column in *The Citizen* on the 25 March 1998. *Courtesy of Gloucestershire Newspapers Ltd.*

teachers are now employed by local education authorities and most are locally organised within a Traveller Education Service (TES). In addition to teachers, TES also employ significant numbers of Classroom Assistants and Education Welfare Officers. Most TES operate as peripatetic teams and over the years these have established effective and functional networks which facilitate co-operation and liaison between authorities and allow for the exchange of information to aid continuity of provision for the Gypsy and Traveller pupils. The vast majority of these posts are supported by what is known as a Section 488 grant made available to local authorities by central government. The specific grant currently supports 65 per cent of the costs involved. In 1999/2000 this grant will support total expenditure in excess of £13 million. This is allocated within the framework of a competitive bidding process with local projects being planned for three year periods at a time.

Gypsy and Traveller children who have been settled in housing for two or more years are not eligible for support under this programme. This is known as the 'Two Year Rule' and is not helpful in some circumstances where the educational difficulties of some of the children concerned, are equal to, if not more extreme, than those of some of the children still 'on the road' and or living in caravans.

A number of voluntary bodies are active in the area of Gypsy and Traveller education. In addition, many professional teachers are members of the National Association of Teachers of Travellers (NATT). This organisation has made a significant contribution to Gypsy and Traveller education over the years by holding a bi-annual national conference together with regular meetings which have a strong in-service training element, and generally in the promotion of good practice and the constructive use of grants made available under the European Commission's Socrates educational programme.

The pioneering and proactive work of TES all over the country has made a real change in the educational opportunities of Gypsy and Traveller children in terms of access and attendance. There are Traveller Education Services in 130 LEAs. Within England, over 17,000 Traveller children receive direct educational support from these services. Over 3,500 schools are supported by peripatetic staff working within TES.

Despite this progress, there are still serious concerns over attendance and achievement. The report published by the Office for Standards in

Education (OFSTED) in March 1996 painted a grim picture, particularly on the issue of attendance :

> Approximately half of Travelling pupils enrolled at primary schools have an attendance rate of 80 per. One-third have a rate between 50 per cent and 79 per cent, with approximately one fifth falling below 49 per cent. This profile is in contrast to that which obtains at the secondary phase. Within the same three categories used above, only about one third of the much smaller number of Travelling pupils enrolled have an attendance rate above 80 per cent, a further third averages between 50 per cent and 79 per cent and with the rest below 49 per cent.

The same report went on to give worrying detail surrounding secondary education:

> It is estimated that only between 15 per cent and 20 per cent of Traveller pupils are registered, or in regular attendance at Key Stage 3 (11-14 years). The number of pupils who continue to Key Stage 4 (14-16 years) shows a further significant decline to an estimated 5 per cent of the secondary cohort.

The report suggests that as many as 10,000 children of secondary school age are not even registered with schools.

In response to this serious situation, the Department for Education and Employment commissioned the making of a video film for Gypsy and Traveller parents, to encourage them to send their children to secondary school. It is entitled *Are We Missing Out*. Research has also been commissioned to explore the reasons for the under-achievement of many Gypsy Traveller pupils.

While, in the main, access to schools has been secured, there are still too many schools where prejudice against Gypsies and Travellers continues in many subtle and unsubtle ways. This appears to be an endemic problem and one identified in the OFSTED report and other official reports and publications. The 1985 Swann report *Education for All* had a section on the educational needs of Travellers children. It talks of the extreme hostility which the Traveller community faces from the settled community:

> The degree of hostility towards Gypsies and other Travellers children if they do enter school is quite remarkable even when set alongside the racism encountered by children from other ethnic minority groups.

There is no shortage of examples of racist attitudes and behaviour towards Gypsy and Traveller children. A survey in Sheffield found that racist name calling was what the Traveller children most hated about going to school. In 1994, in a school in the West London area, Gypsy children were subjected to name calling and attacks. Gorgio children blocked the school gate and prevented them leaving school and going home until the police were called. On another occasion the provoked Gypsy children retaliated. Three Gypsy children were suspended but no Gorgio children were punished. In a school in Hackney a playground argument started between an Afro-Caribbean pupil and a Gypsy girl. Each descended into racist abuse of the other. The Gypsy girl was excluded from the school for making racist remarks – the other girl remained on the roll. In 1998 a school in Gloucestershire admitted four infant Gypsy children. The next day 150 parents kept their children out of school and a local newspaper ran a headline, 'Would you like your child to sit next to a Gypsy?'

Despite these unacceptable stories of racist intolerance, progress is being made. The progress made, though, has represented a long up-hill struggle and it is certain that countless generations of Gypsy and Traveller children have needlessly lost out on their legal entitlement to formal education. There is the need for an official apology to be made to the victims.

9

Civil rights and international action

Self-representation: The Gypsy Council

Norman Dodds and his Gypsy friends (see Chapter 5) were not alone in their struggle. In Dorset, Romany activist Tom Jonell campaigned from 1963, the year in which Tom O'Doherty, an Irish Traveller, founded the Society of Travelling People in Leeds.

Two years later, Richard Hauser of the Centre for Group Studies and his wife, the pianist Hephzibah Menuhin, hosted a meeting which was the first step in changing the face of the Gypsy political scene in Britain. Those present included Vaida Voevod of the Communauté Mondiale Gitane (see below), David Smith (author of several reports on Gypsies) and Brian Richardson, active in the National Council for Civil Liberties. During 1966, Grattan Puxon, a journalist who had been drawn into the fight for Travellers' Rights in Ireland, returned to England. He drew together Gypsies, such as John Brazil and Joe Eastwood, and their Gorgio supporters who later that same year took a lead in setting up the Gypsy Council. The names of thirty Gypsies were on a leaflet calling all Travellers to come to a meeting in Kent on 11 December 1966 to support the following demands:

- camping sites
- equal rights to education, work and houses
- equal standing through respect between ourselves and our settled neighbours.

An additional twist was that the venue, the Bull's Head, was a public house which had a 'No Gypsies' sign on the front, a fact of which the press made much. The new Gypsy Council was to thrive on media publicity.

Over the next two years, Puxon and other leaders of the Council and their Gorgio sympathisers were to run a campaign of passive resistance to evictions of caravans which hit the press and TV screen. Puxon himself drew inspiration from Gandhi's 'passive resistance' and the movement to drive the British out of India, while experience of CND and the anti-Vietnam demonstrations either in person or as a TV viewer was common to all.

People from all walks of life supported the campaign for stopping places and education. Links were forged between Gypsies and Gorgios and a 'bust card' was printed which, at its peak had twenty-three phone numbers across Britain for calling in an emergency. At the first sign of a bailiff arriving to evict from an unofficial site a Gypsy would run to the nearest public telephone and a mixture of housewives, pastors and students would assemble with the Gypsies, making a human barrier between their caravans and the council officials with their accompanying police and towing vehicles. This passive resistance was a major factor in persuading the Government to take some action over the 'Gypsy problem', culminating in the 1968 Caravan Sites Act.

The battle for sites wound down during the 1970s for a number of reasons. Many of the most obstinate local councils opened sites, splits within the Gypsy Council weakened its leadership and the fact that caravans were becoming more expensive meant that their owners were no longer willing to risk damage during an eviction but were inclined to move off at the first sight of bailiffs. More recently, Gypsies and New Travellers have not meekly accepted the new laws on trespass in the 1994 Criminal Justice Act and have resisted evictions on many occasions in different parts of Britain.

Realignments within the Gypsy civil rights movement led to the formation of the Romany Guild in 1972 which merged with the Gypsy Council to become the National Gypsy Council in 1974. The Association of Gypsy Organisations was formed in 1975 but no longer operates as an independent organisation, having merged with the NGEC which was renamed the Gypsy Council for Education, Culture, Welfare and Civil Rights. At the time of writing there are also other

'The Battle of Rose Hill' in Merton, south London, one of the violent evictions before the coming into force of site provision for Gypsies under the Caravan Sites Act (1968); *photographer unknown.*

groups with regional rather than national membership. We list the major organisations in an appendix.

The International Movement

In 1959 Ionel Rotaru, a member of the Ursari clan and a writer, adopting the old chieftain's title Vaida Voevod, emerged in Paris as would-be leader of the world's Gypsies. He founded an international organisation Communauté Mondiale Gitane (CMG). This was banned by the French Government in 1965 but Vanko Rouda and other ex-members of the CMG then formed a new movement, the Comité International Tzigane (CIT). As they did not register it officially, the French Government has not been able to dissolve it. Grattan Puxon and the Dublin-based Itinerant Action Group were in contact with both the CMG and the CIT, and Vanko Rouda spoke at the foundation meeting of the Gypsy Council.

In 1971, the Gypsy Council was host to the First World Romany Congress held in the premises of a boarding school near London. The CIT, now called the Comité International Rom, was active in mustering support for this meeting which was attended by delegates and observers from over fourteen countries. At the Congress there emerged a flag (blue and green with a red wheel), an anthem (*Gelem, gelem* – we travelled) and five commissions which were to meet between congresses.

The Second Congress was held in Geneva in 1978 with 120 delegates and observers from twenty-six countries. The link with India was a predominant theme of this congress which opened with the presentation by W. R. Rishi from Chandigarh of a symbolic package of earth from the historical mother country of the Romanies. New statutes were elaborated and a fresh organisation emerged, the International Romany Union, which was to operate between congresses and which in the following year gained recognition from UNESCO.

The Third Congress was held in Göttingen, Germany, in 1981, with even larger numbers, some 300 delegates and observers. Prominence was given to recalling the Nazi period. Invited Jewish speakers included Simon Wiesenthal and Richard Hauser. A new demand was made for global reparations from the German government. This has not yet been met but Bonn does now support the national German Sinti (Gypsy) Union based in Heidelberg. An international Presidium or committee was elected with Peter Mercer as the British member.

As the frontiers of Eastern Europe began to open up, the Fourth Congress in 1990 was held near Warsaw in Poland. Over 300 persons from twenty countries attended, including important delegations from Bulgaria, Czechoslovakia, Romania and the Soviet Union. It was decided to set up commissions to produce a standard Romani literary language and an encyclopaedia. Through lack of financing these tasks are being undertaken by working parties attached to the Centre de Recherches Tsiganes in Paris and largely funded from the European Union in Brussels. The Congress reaffirmed the Indian origin of the Romanies while recognising that they would remain citizens of the countries where they now live. The British and Irish delegations stressed the need for caravan sites and education.

The Romany Union took part in setting up a new overall international body on which all Gypsy organisations can be represented – the

Standing Conference for Co-operation and Co-ordination of Romani Associations in Europe. This was founded on July 30, 1994, in Strasbourg. There have been meetings at various locations, including Vienna in November 1996, which discussed the rise of anti-Gypsyism in Europe.

As we go to press, there are plans for a fifth Congress in the Netherlands in the year 2000.

European Organisations –
The Council of Europe

The Council of Europe covers over thirty countries. It has no powers over its members and has until now had a low profile in countries such as Britain. Nevertheless, it has played a part in raising consciousness of the Gypsy issue at international level. As early as 1969 the Consultative Assembly made a recommendation that member states should try and improve the conditions of life of their Gypsy citizens.

In 1975, the Committee of Ministers of the Council, noting that nothing had been done by member states as a result of the above mentioned recommendation, passed a strongly worded resolution. It called for an end to discrimination, the safeguarding of the culture of nomadic populations, the building of caravan sites and encouraging the education of children and adults.

The Parliamentary Assembly of the Council of Europe of 1993 proposed a number of measures in its Recommendation 1203. These covered a range of issues from culture to civil rights. Again, the Council has no power to enforce these proposals.

The Council financed and published a most useful survey on Gypsies in all the member states, *Gypsies and Travellers*, of which a second edition came out in 1998. Meetings for teachers and others involved in education have been held in Donaueschingen and elsewhere and reports of the discussions and conclusions have been circulated. It initiated a project for the history of minorities, including Gypsies, to be included in the history textbooks and teaching programmes of member states.

In 1995, the Council established a new advisory body – the Specialist Group on Roma/Gypsies (Mg-S-Rom). The seven original members of the group came from Finland, Spain, Netherlands, Romania,

Bulgaria, Italy and Poland. The latter was represented by the Romany activist Andrzej Mirga.

European Convention on Human Rights

A number of Gypsies in England who have been refused planning permission on appeal to Inspectors from the Planning Agency have taken their case to the European Court of Human Rights. They claim that their right to a home has been denied contrary to Article 8 of the European Convention on Human Rights, which came into force in 1953 and which states:

- Everyone has the right to respect for his private and family life, his home and his correspondence.
- There shall be no interference by a public authority with the exercise of this right except such as is in accordance with the law and is necessary in a democratic society in the interests of national security, public safety or the economic well-being of the country, for the prevention of disorder or crime, for the protection of health or morals, or for the protection of the rights and freedoms of others.

In the case of Mrs Buckley of Cambridgeshire, she alleged that the planning system effectively made it impossible for her to pursue her way of life as a Romany Gypsy, as her only other available option was to move onto an unsuitable pitch on a public site. In January 1995 the European Commission (which until this year vetted ECHR claims) concluded by 5 votes to 4 that her Article 8 rights had been breached; however, in September 1996 the European Court of Human Rights took the opposite view.

Central to the Court's reasoning was that the state had not employed disproportionate means to enforce planning control (as Mrs Buckley was subject only to 'small fines'). Other cases in which eviction action and worse are employed, or where non-planning options and personal circumstances are more problematic, might yet succeed. Anyone professionally involved in such a case needs to read the complete Buckley judgement.

Mrs Buckley's case began before the abolition of the 1968 Caravan Sites Act. Other cases are now working their way through the long and complicated legal procedures. On 4th March 1998 the European Commission of Human Rights considered a number of cases regarding Gypsies who had their own piece of land. They declared as admissible the applications of Mr and Mrs Coster of Maidstone, Mr and Mrs Beard and three others. In each case there was a lack of alternative sites in the area. The results of these appeals to the Court are awaited with interest, although in the case of Mr and Mrs Coster, they have already been driven off their site by enforcement proceedings and accepted housing.

The coming into force of the Human Rights Act 1998 on October 2nd 2000 will bring about the incorporation of the Convention into British law, and many people will no longer have to undertake the long pilgrimage to Strasbourg to find a remedy for breaches of their rights. The Act will enable anyone involved in legal proceedings, at any level from Magistrates Court to the House of Lords and including Social Security and other Tribunals, whether criminal or civil proceedings, to invoke their rights where relevant. The Act makes it unlawful for any public authority to act in a way which is, and for any other law to be, incompatible with the Convention.

Recent cuts in legal aid mean that some people who need protection for their rights will be unable to afford to enforce them, and it has been mooted by some legal commentators that the Act will not represent a revolution until and unless the judiciary are more rights-minded and less fearful of being too powerful in relation to the government. Nonetheless, a more immediate and domestic remedy for the breach of rights is to be welcomed, and local authorities and the police will have to conduct a review all of their working practices and procedures to ensure that they are fair, balanced, and "necessary in a democratic society". The days of police raids on Gypsy sites involving 200 officers, ninety-five Gypsies, and one resulting arrest, for example, may well be numbered.

European organisations –
The European Union

As early as 1981 members of the Romany Union first approached the European Community (as it was then called) to press the case for aiding Gypsies. There was a delay until 1984 when the European Parliament decided to study school provision. Information was collected from all member countries and published in 1987.

At the end of the study there were forty-three recommendations. They are farsighted and include:

- That teaching material incorporating elements of Gypsy and Traveller culture, language and history be developed.
- That Travellers be employed as paid assistants in connection with the schooling of their children.

Needs other than education were not forgotten: 'Nomadism must be officially recognised and provision made for nomads.'

The study was accepted by the Education Committee and has been published in many of the European Union languages. Since then, a number of meetings of teachers and educationalists, as well as representatives of the Gypsies, have been held, and the study has been enlarged to cover Spain and Portugal. A new edition was published in 1998 (see Liégois in bibliography). Gypsies await further positive action in the form of pressure on governments to provide a framework within which their children can receive education, as well as finance for adult training programmes.

This may come about as a result of resolutions on the general situation of the Romanies passed by the Council of Ministers in 1989 and reaffirmed by the Parliament in 1994. (see Appendix 4)

A positive development has been the work of the Centre for Gypsy Research in Paris under the direction of Jean-Pierre Liegeois. Projects funded wholly or partly by the European Union include a newsletter (*Interface*), three working parties (on language, history and education) and support for a series of publications.

The Union has warned Bulgaria and the Czech Republic in particular that, under the Association Agreements for new states entering the Union, they need to make more effort to integrate their Romany populations if they are to be admitted to the Union.

By way of conclusion

As you read these words, over 3,000 families are living on the roadside, on the edge of a sewage farm or perhaps encamped on your local sports field. They have no water supply or rubbish collection and the children are probably not attending any school.

The 1968 Caravan Sites Act provided the means by which these families could be given places where they could legally stop while still preserving their independent way of life. Sites are the first step to health and education – and education is one of the means by which Gypsies will become more and more able to stand up for themselves against officialdom and bureaucracy.

The 1968 Act has been repealed and voluntary site provision will never catch up with the birth rate, not until councillors risk losing votes and permit sites in their area, and the residents, i.e. the general public, become more knowledgeable and able to distinguish the reality about Gypsies from the myths.

All Gypsies, whether on sites or not, suffer from discrimination and harassment. The Race Relations and Public Order Acts should protect them.

We hope that the information in the preceding pages will help to dispel some of the misunderstandings about Gypsies and create a better climate of opinion in which they may integrate, without being assimilated, into the Europe of the new millennium.

Appendices

Appendix 1
Addresses and websites

Addresses

Advisory Council for the Education of Romany and other Travellers, Moot House, The Stow, Harlow, Essex CM20 3AG.

Department of the Environment, Transport and the Regions, Gypsy Sites Branch, 2/A1 Eland House, Bressenden Place, London SW1E 5DU.

East Anglian Gypsy Council, Plot 3, Travellers Site, Oxney Road, Peterborough, Cambridgeshire PE1 5NX.

European Federation for the Education of the Children of the Occupational Travellers (EFECOT), Grensstraat 6, B-1210 Brussels, Belgium

Enabler Publications / Alan Dearling (publishers and booksellers), 3 Russell House, Lym Close, Lyme Regis, Dorset DT7 3DE.

Friends, Families and Travellers Support Group (FFT), Community Base, Queens Road, Brighton, East Sussex.

Gypsy Council for Education, Culture, Welfare and Civil Rights, 8 Hall Road, Aveley, Essex RM15 4HD.

International Association of Gypsies in Professional Occupations (IAGPO), c/o John Day, 7 Travellers Site, Oxney Road, Peterborough PE1 5NX.

Irish Travellers' Project, Brent Irish Advisory Services (BIAS), 90 High Street, Harrow-on-the-Hill, Middlesex HA1 3LP

Labour Campaign for Travellers' Rights, 84 Bankside Street, Leeds LS8 5AD.

National Association of Gypsy and Traveller Officers, c/o Hampshire County Council, The Castle, Winchester, Hampshire SO23 9DS.

National Association of Gypsy Women, Meadowview, Goldsmith Drive, Lower Holbridge Road, Rayleigh, Essex.

National Association of Health Workers with Travellers, c/o Balsall Heath Health Centre, 43 Edward Road, Balsall Heath, Birmingham B12 9LB.

National Association of Teachers of Travellers, c/o The Graiseley Centre, Pool
Street, Wolverhampton WV2 4NE.

National Gypsy Council, Greenacres Caravan Park, Hapsford, Helsby,
Warrington, Cheshire WA6 OJS.

National Romani Rights Association. 8 Reid Way, King's Lynn, Norfolk
PE30 2LL.

Romanestan Publications (publishers and booksellers), 22 Northend, Warley,
Brentwood, Essex CM14 5LD.

Romani/Traveller Studies at Newcastle, c/o Colin Clark, Department of Social
Policy, University of Newcastle upon Tyne, Newcastle upon Tyne,
NE1 7RU.

Romani Studies at Greenwich University, School of Social Sciences, University
of Greenwich, Avery Hill Road, London SE1 2UG

Romany Guild, The Urban Farm, 50-52 Temple Mills Lane, London E15.

Traveller Law Research Uni, Cardiff Law School, PO Box 427, Cardiff, Wales
CF1 1XD.

Traveller School Charity, PO Box 36, Grantham, Lincolnshire NG31 6EW.

Web Sites

This list is confined to those web sites specifically related to Gypsies and Travellers in
Britain.

Alan Lodge's Homepage ('Tash' on New Travellers),
http://www.gn.apc.org/tash/

Department of the Environment, Transport and Regions Homepage,
http://www.detr.gov.uk/

Enabler Publications, http://members.aol.com/dearling/enabler/

Gypsy and Traveller Education (UK),
http://www.jokak.demon.co.uk/artemis/homepage.html

Romani Studies at Greenwich University, http://www.gre.ac.uk/~at02/

Scottish Traveller Education Project, http://www.mhie.ac.uk/~step/

The National Association of Health Workers with Travellers,
http://nahwt.supernews.com/

The Patrin (section on Great Britain),
http://www.geocities.com/~patrin/countries.htm#GreatBritain

University of Hertfordshire Press,
http://www.herts.ac.uk/UHPress/Gypsies.html

University of Liverpool Gypsy Collections Homepage,
http://sca.lib.liv.ac.uk/collections/gypsy/intro.htm

Web Homepage of Traveller-acad e-mail discussion list,
http://www.mailbase.ac.uk/lists/traveller-acad/

Appendix 2
Bibliography and further reading

ACTON, *Thomas. Gypsy politics and social chan*ge. London: Routledge, Kegan
     Paul, 1974.

ACTON, Thomas. (Ed.) *Gypsy politics and Traveller Identity.* Hatfield: University
     of Hertfordshire Press, 1997.

ACTON, Thomas and MUNDY, Gary (Ed.) *Romani culture and Gypsy identity.*
     Hatfield: University of Hertfordshire Press, 1997.

ADAMS, B. and others. *Gypsies and government policy in England.* London:
     Heinemann, 1975.

CARDIFF UNIVERSITY SCHOOL OF EDUCATION. *Traveller children and
     educational need in Wales.* Cardiff, 1998.

CENTRE FOR GYPSY RESEARCH. *The education of Gypsy and Traveller
     Children: action research and co-ordination.* Hatfield: University of
     Hertfordshire Press, 1993.

DALEY, Ian and HEDERSON, Jo. *Static life on the site.* Yorkshire Art Circus, 1998.

EARLE, F. and others. *A time to travel: An introduction to Britain's newer Travellers.*
     Lyme Regis: Enabler Publications, 1994.

DEARLING, A. *Almost everything you need to know about the Travellers' School
     Charity,* Lyme Regis: Enabler Publications, December 1997.

DEARLING, A. *No boundaries.* Lyme Regis: Enabler Publications, 1998.

FORRESTER, Bill *The Travellers' handbook.* London: Interchange Books, 1985.

FRASER, Angus. *The Gypsies.* Oxford: Blackwell, 1992.

FRIENDS, FAMILIES AND TRAVELLERS SUPPORT GROUP. *Planning
     appeals and Gypsies and Travellers.* (Results of a study of planning appeal
     decision letters). Glastonbury: FFTSG, 1998.

HANCOCK, Ian and others. *The Roads of the Roma.* A PEN anthology of Gypsy
     writers. Hatfield: University of Hertfordshire Press, 1998.

HAWES, Derek. Gypsies, *Travellers and the Health Service*. Bristol: Policy
        Press,1997.

HAWES, Derek and PEREZ, Barbara. *The Gypsy and the State: the ethnic cleansing of
        British society.* Bristol: Policy Press, (2nd edn)1996.

KENRICK, Donald. Gypsies: *From India to the Mediterranean.* The Interface
        Collection, Volume 3 Toulouse: CRDP, 1993.

KENRICK, Donald. *Historical Dictionary of the Gypsies (Romanies),* Lanham, Md:
        Scarecrow Press, 1998.

KENRICK, Donald and PUXON, Grattan. *Gypsies under the Swastika.* Interface
        Collection, Volume 8. Hatfield: University of Hertfordshire Press, 1995.

LEBLON, Bernard. *Gypsies and flamenco,* The Interface Collection, Volume 6.
        Hatfield: University of Hertfordshire Press, 1995.

LIEGEOIS, J-P. *Gypsies.* London: Al-Saaqi, 1986.

LIEGEOIS, J-P. *School provision for ethnic minorities: the Gypsy Paradigm,*
        The Interface Collection, Volume 11. Hatfield: University of
        Hertfordshire Press, 1998.

LIEGEOIS, J-P. Roma, *Gypsies, Travellers,* Council of Europe, 1995.

LOWE, R. and SHAW, W. Travellers, *Voices of the New Age Nomads,* London:
        Fourth Estate, 1993.

MCKAY, G. *Senseless acts of beauty: cultures of resistance since the sixties,*
        London: Verso.

MAYALL, David. *English Gypsies and State Poicies.* The Interface Collection,
        Volume 7. Hatfield: University of Hertfordshire Press, 1995.

MORRIS, Rachel and CLEMENTS, Luke (Eds). *Gaining ground: law reform for
        Gypsies and Travellers.* Hatfield: University of Hertfordshire Press, 1999.

NAYLOR, Sally and WILD-SMITH, Kanta *Broadening horizons – education and
        travelling children.* Essex County Council, 1997

NEAT, T, *The summer walkers: travelling people and pearl-fishers in the Highlands of
        Scotland,* Edinburgh: Canongate Books, 1998.

NINER, Pat and others. *Local authority powers for managing unauthorised camping.*
        Research report. London: Dept of the Environment, 1998.

OFFICE FOR STANDARDS IN EDUCATION. *The Education of Travelling
        Children.* London, 1996.

OFFICE FOR STANDARDS IN EDUCATION. *Raising the achievement of minori-
        ty ethnic pupils.* London. 1999.

OKELY, J. *The Traveller-Gypsies.* Cambridge: Cambridge University Press, 1983.

REHFISCH, A and REHFISCH, F. 'Scottish Travellers or Tinkers', in Rehfisch
        (Ed.) *Gypsies, tinkers and other Travellers,* London: Academic Press, 1975.

REISS, C. *Education of Gypsy children.* London: Macmillan, 1975.

SANDFORD, J. *Gypsies.* London: Sphere, 1973. New edition to be published by
        University of Hertfordshire Press as *Rokkering with the Gorjios.*

SCOTTISH ASSOCIATION OF HEALTH COUNCILS. *Health care and travelling people: A charter for health and travelling people*, September 1992.

SCOTTISH OFFICE CENTRAL RESEARCH UNIT. *Counting Travellers in Scotland: the 1992 Picture*, Edinburgh, 1993.

STANGROOME, V. *New Nomadic Groups: an information pack on the New Age Traveller phenomenon*. Self-published, 1993.

WILSON, Mark. *A directory of planning policies for Gypsy site provision in England*. Bristol: Policy Press, 1998.

YOUNG, Mike. *Unwanted Journey. Why Central European Roma are fleeing to the UK*. London: Refugee Council, 1999.

DoE Circulars

1/94 *Gypsy Sites and Planning*

18/94 *Gypsy Sites Policy and Unauthorised Camping*

DETR and Home Office. *Managing Unauthorised Camping. A Good Practice Guide*. London: DETR, 1998.

Appendix 3
Chronology

1959 *Highways Act* (legislated against Gypsies parking-up on laybys).

1960 *Caravan Sites and Control of Development Act* (controlled private sites).
   Commons Act (stopped camping on commons).

1966 Gypsy Council founded.

1968 *Caravan Sites Act* (see 1970 below). Ministry of Housing Circular
   49/68 explains the Act.

1970 Part 2 of the *Caravan Sites Act* comes into operation (Councils must provide sites for Gypsies).

1972 First 'designations' under the 1968 Act.

1976 *Race Relations Act* (bans discrimination).

1977 Cripps Report.
   Housing (Homeless Persons) Act (Gypsies with no legal pitch can be count-
   ed as homeless).
   Department of the Environment Circular 28/77 (temporary proposals
   until Cripps Report has been studied).
   Croydon refuses a school place to a Gypsy on an illegal site.

1978 Circular 57/78 (following up Cripps Report).

1980 Offence of 'being a Gypsy encamping on a highway' abolished.
   Education Act (Gypsies on illegal sites are entitled to a school place).

1981 Brymbo discrimination case.

1985 Rafferty and Gilhaney cases (a county cannot evict Gypsies without
   providing an alternative site).
   New Travellers at Stonehenge.

1986 Statutory Instrument 1986/2289 (reduces to two days the period for
   giving a trespasser notice to quit).
   *Public Order Act (*Trespass on vacant land becomes a criminal offence;
   reinforces law on racial harassment).

1987   Wibberley Review (of the 1968 Act).
         CRE v.Dutton. First hearing (see below).
         Trespass clauses of the *Public Order Act* come into operation.
1988   Greenwich v. Powell, House of Lords (Confirms Gypsies can be evicted
         without notice from council sites and defines 'Gypsy'.)
         CRE v. Dutton (Appeal court hearing), No Travellers notices are indi-
         rect discrimination.
         Education Reform Act. New fund for Traveller education in England and
         Wales.
1990   4th World Romany Congress, Warsaw.
1994   *Criminal Justice and Public Order Act* (New trespass laws, repeal of
         Caravans Site Act of 1968).
1998   Circular on Good Practice in Evictions.

Appendix 4
Resolutions by
international bodies

On the situation of Gypsies in the Community.
On 21 April 1994 a major resolution was passed by the European
Parliament. The Parliament

1. Calls on the governments of the Member States to introduce legal, admin-
    istrative and social measures to improve the social situation of Gypsies and
    Travelling People in Europe;
2. Calls for all citizens of non-member countries legally residing in a Member
    State, including Gypsies, to have the same rights to travel throughout the
    European Union as citizens of the Union;
3. Recommends that the Governments of the Member States add an addition-
    al protocol on minorities to the European Convention of Human Rights, in
    which the definition of minorities explicitly includes Gypsies in the form
    of a reference to landless minorities;
4. Calls on the Commission and the Council of Europe to draw up a general
    report on the situation of Gypsies in the Member States, with particular
    regard to coercive measures taken by states, human rights violations, etc.;
5. Recommends that the Commission and Council adopt initiatives in the
    fields of culture, education, information and equal rights, in the form of
    proposals to the governments or the appropriate local and regional author-
    ities of the Member States;
6. Urges that budget items be maintained, and wherever possible increased, in
    the Community budget for funding such social, cultural and educational
    action for the Gypsy community;
7. Recommends that the Commission, the Council and the governments of
    the Member States should do everything in their power to assist in the eco-
    nomic, social and political integration of Gypsies, with the objective of

eliminating the deprivation and poverty in which the great majority of
Europe's Gypsy population still lives at the present time;

8. Recognises that Gypsies are subject to persecution in many countries in
central and eastern Europe and therefore recommends the EU Member
States should take great care when examining applications for asylum by
Gypsies from these countries;

9. Condemns the conclusion of repatriation agreements between the Member
States of the European Union and the countries of central and eastern
Europe which result in refugees being traded like goods;

10. Stresses the need for fresh measures in the educational field, if racism and
xenophobia are to be combated effectively, and urges the Commission, the
Council and the governments of the Members States to promote a range of
measures to help remove the major obstacles to the school education of the
children of Gypsies and Travelling People;

11. Calls on the Commission, the Council and the governments of the Member
States to recognise the language and other aspects of Gypsy culture as
forming an integral part of Europe's cultural heritage;

12. Recommends that the Commission and the Council carry out an in-depth
study of the education and training problems facing Gypsies and nomads,
particularly the schooling of Gypsy children who do not have an adequate
knowledge of the language of the country or of the region in which they
reside; also recommends setting up a specific training programme designed
to enable teaching in the Romani language to be included in curricula, and,
as part of its work in the field of inter-cultural education, to prepare information sheets on the subject for teachers;

13. Reminds the Commission, the Council and the governments of the
Member States of the decisive role of the media and of local and regional
authorities in eliminating racial prejudice and supports full co-operation
with the Economic and Social Committee, the Council of Europe and the
CSCE to ensure that problems linked to racism and xenophobia are tackled
effectively;

14. Urges the Commission and the Member States to implement programmes
which provide adequate information for the general public on genuine culture, especially by promoting information programmes carried out by
Gypsies themselves;

15. Reminds the Community's Gypsy citizens of their rights to submit petitions to the European Parliament if they believe themselves to have been
the victims of racist behaviour;

16. Calls on the German Government to compensate any Gypsies and their
families who were victims of Nazi persecution;

17. Calls on the Member States not to expel any Gypsies who have fled

Romania and the former Yugoslavia and to facilitate the entry of their family members;

18. Urges the Commission and the Council to set up a European research and
    information centre, through which the most representative Gypsy organi-
    sations could deal with the Community authorities on all political, social,
    or cultural matters involving Gypsies;

19. Encourages Gypsy organisations to amalgamate at European level, and
    calls on the Commission and the Member States to give financial assistance
    to such an amalgamation;

20. Instructs its President to forward this resolution to the Council, the
    Commission and the governments of the Member States.
    Extracts are given below from other earlier important international resolu-
    tions concerning Gypsies. Fuller texts can be found in Marielle Danbakli,
    On Gypsies: Texts Issued by International Institutions (Toulouse: CRDP,
    1994).

The Social Situation of Nomads in Europe
The Resolution of 22 May, 1975, of the Committee of Ministers of the
Council of Europe.

All necessary measures within the framework of national legislation should be
taken to stop any form of discrimination against nomads.

Camping and residence of nomads on camping sites equipped so as to promote
safety, hygiene and welfare should be facilitated and encouraged.

Nomads and their children should be enabled to benefit effectively from the various existing provisions for vocational guidance, training and retraining.

Prevention of Discrimination and Protection of Minorities
The Resolution of 31 August, 1977, of the Sub-Commission (of the
Economic and Social Council of the United Nations)

The Sub-Commission appeals to those countries which have Gypsies
(Romanies) within their borders to accord to these people, if they have not
yet done so, all the rights that are enjoyed by the rest of the population.

On Stateless Nomads and
Nomads of Undetermined Nationality
Recommendation of 22 February, 1983, of the Committee of Ministers of
the Council of Europe

Each state should take appropriate steps to facilitate in relation to stateless
nomads or nomads of undetermined nationality [entering or on its

territory] the establishment of a link with the state concerned.

On the situation of Gypsies in the Community
Resolution of 24 May, 1984, of the European Parliament (of the European Communities)

The Parliament calls on the government of Member States to eliminate any discriminatory provisions which may still exist in their legislation, to co-ordinate their approach to the reception of Gypsies, to make it easier for nomads to attach themselves to a State, and to draw up programmes to be subsidised from Community funds aimed at improving the situation of Gypsies.

On School Provision for Gypsy and Traveller Children
Resolution of 22 May, 1989 of the Council of the European Communities

The Council and the Ministers for Education will strive to promote support for educational establishments, experiments with distance learning, the training and employment of teachers of Romany or Traveller origin wherever possible, the encouragement of research on the culture, history and language of Gypsies and Travellers.

Resolution of 19 August, 1991, of the Sub-Commission (of the Economic and Social Council of the United Nations)

The Sub-Commission, aware of the fact that, in many countries various obstacles exist to the full realisation by persons belonging to the Romany community of their civil, political, economic, social and cultural rights, invites States which have Romany communities living within their borders to take, in consultation with those communities, all the necessary legislative, administrative, economic and social measures to ensure the de jure and de facto equality of the members of those communities and to guarantee their protection and security.

Protection of Romanies (Gypsies)
Resolution of 4 March, 1992, of the Commission on Human Rights (of the Economic and Social Council of the United Nations)

The Commission requests the Special Rapporteur of the Subcommission on the Prevention of Discrimination and Protection of Minorities to accord special attention to and to provide information on the specific conditions in which the Romanies (Gypsies) live.

It invites States to adopt all appropriate measures in order to eliminate any form of discrimination against Romanies (Gypsies).

On Gypsies in Europe.

Recommendation of 2 February, 1993, of the Parliamentary Assembly of the Council of Europe.

The Assembly recommends that the Committee of Ministers initiate the following measures:

Introduce the teaching and study of Gypsy music at several schools of music in Europe.

Special attention should be paid to the education of women and mothers with their younger children.

Member states should ratify the 4th Protocol to the European Convention on Human Rights which guarantees freedom of movement and is, as such, essential for travellers.

A mediator for Gypsies should be appointed by the Council of Europe.

Appendix 5
Travellers, Gypsies and the Media: a good practice guide from the Commission for Racial Equality

Coverage of race and ethnic issues across the media has significantly improved over the past twenty years. There has been a wider and more constructive exploration of many questions and a reduction in the use of language that is offensive to members of different ethnic groups. However many problems remain. These recommendations are designed to help in dealing with one of them: the way parts of the media report on Traveller and/or Gypsy issues.

Poor quality reporting which exploits or panders to stereotypes can cause much hurt to those about whom the stories are written. By repeating false and negative stereotypes the media can encourage bad practice on the part of those with whom Travellers and Gypsies deal and can validate the expression of language and attitudes which in any other circumstances would be seen as totally unacceptable.

The Commission for Racial Equality has handled cases under the Race Relations Act for Travellers and Gypsies for over twenty years. The number of such cases continues to run at several dozen each year. The majority of these cases involve clear breaches of the Act.

These guidelines are not intended to make the media shy away from covering issues and stories to do with Travellers and Gypsies. Quite the contrary. The CRE and those organisations representing Travellers and Gypsies want to see more coverage in the media but are keen to help the media develop a coverage that is honest and fair, open and inclusive.

Steer clear of exploiting prejudice

The public wants a media that is campaigning, but those campaigns should be built on matters of genuine public concern, not simply prejudices against particular groups.

Check the facts

Go to the experts who can help to set the context. With these recommendations we include a list of contacts of individuals and organisations which can help you with various aspects of your story. 196 Make sure that wherever possible you check the details with a relevant source and don't just rely on expressions of local or popular prejudice. Many allegations are made about Travellers, Gypsies and now Roma asylum seekers from Eastern Europe, but can those making the allegations actually substantiate them?

Don't let your new agenda be driven by the way others are handling the issue

Certain story lines easily dominate media discussion of Travellers or Gypsies while issues of great importance to the communities involved are downplayed or ignored altogether. Don't write about Travellers and Gypsies only in the context of disputes over stopping places, look also at the problems Travellers face.

Look behind the story line

Don't assume there is only one point of view. Always seek the views of Traveller and Gypsy organisations to see whether or not there is an alternative interpretation or a different and more significant story line to be presented.

Listen to the people you are writing about

This is particularly important when it comes to the terms and language you use. Terms like 'tinker', 'itinerant' or 'gypo' are all highly offensive to those about whom they are used and should be avoided. The terms Traveller(s), Gypsy or Irish Traveller should be used with initial capital letters. Offensive stereotypes (for example 'scroungers', 'dole dodgers', 'bogus asylum seeker') should only be used when they are accurate descriptions of particular individuals and should not be employed to negatively stereotype whole groups.

Don't label people if it is not relevant

Reference to the fact that an individual is a Traveller, Gypsy or Irish Traveller should only be made when it is relevant and appropriate.

Appendix 6
Gypsy and Traveller languages

Each of the five groups of traditional Gypsies or Travellers has its own language. The Rom and some of the Kalé still speak the Romani language, using its traditional grammar.

Romani died out among the Romany chals early in the twentieth century and has been replaced by a variety of English (known as *poggerdi chib*) using many Romani words.

> The *rakli jelled* to the *gav* to *kin* some *pobbels.*
> [The girl went to the village to buy some apples]

The Irish Travellers used to speak a variety of Irish using many words from vocabularies known as Gammon or Shelta. They now speak a variety of English known as cant, but incorporating the same words. Sometimes a whole sentence will be in the cant.

> *Bug muilsha gather skai.* [Give me a drink of water].

Most Scottish Travellers speak English but again with many words that are not used by the general population. Some of these words are of Romani origin, bearing out the theory that the Scottish Travellers have intermarried with Romany chals over the years.

An example of Lowland Scottish Travellers' cant:

> *Bing avree, gheddie,* and get some *peeve.* [Go out, lad, and get some beer]

The dialect of the Borders is closer to that of the English Romany chals while some of the Highland and Islands Scottish Travellers who travel in the

Highlands and to the Western Isles speak a cant based on Scottish Gaelic. For example:

S'deis sium a' meartsacha air a charan. [We are going on the sea].

The Romani language

The following sketch of European Romani is intended to illustrate the connections with north Indian languages, and to show that it is not just slang or a pidgin but has a grammar. Inflected (grammatical) Romani died out in England late in the nineteenth century and in Wales sometime in the middle of the twentieth century

These examples of Romani words are taken from W.R. Rishi's *Multilingual Romani Dictionary*. Prakrit is a later form of Sanskrit. People who speak Hindi, Punjabi or Gujerati will recognise many common Romani words. Bengali or Sylheti speakers may know a few.

Romani	*Sanskrit / Prakrit*	*English*
byav	vivaha	wedding
kako	kakka	uncle
kalo	kala	black
nakh	nakka	nose
puch	pracch	ask
thuv	dhuma	smoke

kako, kalo, nakh and puch are used in English Romani while 'thuv' survives in the word 'thuvalo' – cigarette.

Romani has a case system not unlike Latin and Classical Greek and, of course, Sanskrit, to which it is related. To give one example, the word for 'boy' changes its endings where English would use a preposition.

raklesa	with a boy
rakleske	to a boy
raklengo	of boys

The verbs change their endings to show the person doing the action and also the time (past, present, future). The verb dikh- (see) takes 32 different endings e.g.

dikhav	I see
dikhlias	he (she) saw

There were three genders (like Latin and German) when the speakers left India, but the neuter disappeared in the Middle East, probably under the influence of Persian. The definite article and adjectives have to change depending on whether they accompany a masculine or feminine noun.

o parno bakro	the white sheep (masculine)
i parni bakri	the white ewe (feminine)
e parne bakre	the white sheep (plural)

University of Hertfordshire Press Books on Gypsies & Travellers

We are the only university press committed to developing a major publishing programme on all aspects of the Romani and other Gypsy people who migrated from north west India during the past fifteen hundred years and are now found in every continent. Our books can be ordered from all good bookshops and by mail order from the publisher at the address given below.

Gaining Ground: Law Reform for Gypsies and Travellers
Rachel Morris and Luke Clements, Traveller Law Research Unit, Cardiff Law School
An agenda for reform in the law, policy and practice relating to Travelling people based on the recommendations of several specialist working parties and two major conferences. Part two, Voices for reform, includes contributions by some of the best known names and organisations active in the field with an Introduction by Lord Avebury.
May 1999. 176 pages, paperback. ISBN 0 900458 98 4. Price: £17.

Gypsy politics and Traveller identity
Edited by Thomas Acton
This book represents the cutting edge of scholarship on how the state deals with Gypsies and Travellers, and how they deal with the state. It includes work by younger writers as well as established Romani Studies scholars such as Nicolae Gheorghe and Donald Kenrick.
May 1997, 174 pages. *Paperback edtion reprinted February 1999*
ISBN 0 900458 75 5 (paperback £14.95); ISBN 0 900458 80 1 (hardback £29.95)

Romani culture and Gypsy identity
Edited by Thomas Acton and Gary Mundy
A genuinely comparative scholarly accounts of Gypsy culture, art and music together with contemporary accounts of changes in education and health which will be an essential part of the knowledge base for anyone working with or studying Gypsies.
Publication: May 1997, 203 pages. Paperback edition reprinted February 1999
ISBN 0 900458 76 3 (paperback £16.95); hardback edition out of print

The education of Gypsy and Traveller Children; action-research and co-ordination

Translated and edited by the Advisory Council for the Education of Romany and other Travellers

This translation of the proceedings of the international conference organised by the Centre for Gypsy Research and held in Carcassonne in 1989 provides a vivid picture of action research into the education of Gypsy and Traveller children in Belgium, France, Germany, Greece, Ireland, Italy, Netherlands, Portugal, Spain and the United Kingdom.

1993, 208pp. ISBN 0 900458 50 X, paperback £12.95

The Roads of the Roma; a PEN anthology of Gypsy writers

Edited by Ian Hancock, Siobhan Dowd and Rajko Djuric

Forty-three poems and prose extracts, most appearing in English for the first time, are arranged alongside an 800-year chronology of repression. What emerges is a portrait of a people struggling to preserve their identity in a hostile world. In his introduction Professor Ian Hancock of the University of Texas, himself an English Gypsy, unravels the history of the Roma since they left their original home in India and traces the growth of a written literature out of an oral tradition.

October 1998, 159 pages. ISBN 0 900458 90 9, paperback £11.99

A way of life

Donn Pohren

Based on Donn Pohren's seven years running a flamenco centre at Morón in Andalusia ("the wildest years of my life which I barely survived") this book gives a vivid unforgettable picture of flamenco when it was still entirely genuine and a part of everyday life.

To be published: September 1999. ISBN 1 902806 03 4. Price: £14.99.

Scholarship and the Gypsy struggle: commitment in Romani studies

Edited by Thomas Acton.

This book of papers by leading scholars on Romani linguistics, folklore, the Porraimos, and the birth of the Romani Congress, etc. is published to celebrate the lifetime achievments of the doyen of committed Romani linguists in Britain, Donald Kenrick.

To be published: June 2000. Paperback. ISBN 1-902806-01-8. Price: £17.95

The Interface Collection

This unique international publishing programmne is managed by the Centre for Gypsy Research of the Université René Descartes, Paris, with the support of the European Commission. The University of Hertfordshire Press is the publisher of English language editions of the *Interface Collection.*

English Gypsies and State Policies

David Mayall (Interface Collection, Volume 7)

This detailed historical study of state policies against Gypsies and its local enforcement throws a new light on our attitudes to more recent immigrants which could be used by teachers for project work into the origins of discrimination against minorities.

September 1995 98pp ISBN 0 900458 64 X, paperback £8.75

Gypsies: from India to the Mediterranean

Donald Kenrick (Interface Collection, Volume 3)

A short readable account of the origin of the Gypsies and the story of their migration over many centuries from India to Europe. Profusely illustrated with engravings and copies of old maps and manuscripts.

CRDP, 1993. ISBN 2 86565 082 0, 63 pages; paperback £7.50

Gypsies in the Ottoman Empire:
a contribution to the history of the Balkans

Elena Marushiakova and Vesselin Popov (Interface Collection).

The Roma presence in the European part of the Ottoman Empire – the Balkans – is centuries old and this region has often been called the second motherland of the Gypsies. From this region Gypsies moved westwards taking with them inherited Balkan cultural models and traditions. It is based on archival sources, mainly detailed tax registers, special laws, guild registers and court documents. Notes on Gypsies in books by foreign travellers are also included.

December 1999. Paperback. ISBN 1 902806 02 6. Price: £9.99.

The Great Gypsy Roundup

Antonio Gomez Alfaro (Interface Collection, Volume 2)

The terrible story of the mass internment without trial of Gypsies in Spain in 1749. The Great Gypsy Roundup has been translated into English from the Spanish and is extensively illustrated with contemporary engravings, maps and manuscripts.

Editoria Gitana, 1995. ISBN 84 87347 12 6, 119 pages; paperback £8.75

A false dawn: my life as a Gypsy woman in Slovakia.

Ilona Lackova, edited by Milena Hübschmannová (Interface Collection, Volume 16)

This remarkable life story transcribed and edited from recordings in Romani gives a vivid picture of life in a prewar Gypsy settlement on the edge of a Slovak village, the terror of the wartime period when the Hlinka guards shaved the heads of the women and forced the men into labour camps and the exhilaration of the Communist period when for a time new opportunities beckoned. The author was the first Gypsy to attend Charles University and became a party official but she also witnessed the destruction of the Romani culture, language and way of life in this false dawn.

October 1999, paperback. ISBN 1-902806-00-X. Price: £11.99.

Gypsies and Flamenco:
the emergence of the art of flamenco in Andalusia
*Bernard Leblon (*Interface Collection, Volume 6)
This greatly expanded new edition on the contribution of the Gypsies of Andalusia to the development of flamenco provides a fuller explanation of some of the technical terms and an invaluable biographical dictionary of the foremost Gypsy flamenco artists of the past.

Spring 2000. ISBN 1 902806 05 0. Price: £11.99

Rokkering to the Gorjios
Compiled and edited by Jeremy Sandford (Interface Collection, Volume 19).
A revised edition of a classic work on Gypsies, which for the first time gave the Gypsies the opportunity to describe the lives they lived in their own words. Lavishly illustrated with stunning period photographs this book reveals a fast vanishing world.

November, 1999. ISBN 1 902806 04 2. Price: £11.99.

Gypsies under the Swastika
Donald Kenrick and Grattan Puxon (Interface Collection, Volume 8)
Contemporary photographs and the deliberate omission of footnotes and references help make it compelling reading for older school children as well as the most comprehensive and up to date single volume account of the fate of the Gypsies in the Holocaust.

November 1995, 157pp. ISBN 0 900458 65 8, paperback £9.75

The Gypsies during the Second World War

Volume 1: From "Race Science" to the Camps
Karola Fings, Herbert Heuss, Frank Sparing Interface Collection, Volume 12
This first volume describes how policies of Gypsy persecution from 1875 onwards led to the establishment of the Race Hygiene Research Centre in 1936 and the policy of extermination of Gypsies on racial grounds before describing the clearing of the cities of Gypsies and the development of the death camps in Nazi Germany at Buchenwald, Ravensbruck and Auschwitz. The suffering and systematic murder of the Gypsies in the Camps is vividly invoked by the eye witness accounts of survivors.

September 1997, 136 pages. ISBN 0 900458 78 X, paperback £12.75.

Volume 2: In the shadow of the Swastika
Interface Collection, Volume 13
Edited by Donald Kenrick
This second volume covers the persecution of the Romanies and Sinti in some of the countries occupied by Germany or ruled by its fascist allies including France, Italy, Austria and the present Czech Republic, Bulgaria, Romania, the Soviet Union and the Baltic States.

March 1999, 220 pages. ISBN 0 900458 85 2, paperback, price £12.75

The Interface Collection – *Reference Documents*

The Interface Collection – *Reference Documents*

School provision for Ethnic Minorities: The Gypsy Paradigm

Professor Jean-Pierre Liégeois, Centre for Gypsy Research, Université René Descartes, Paris.
(Interface Collection, Volume 11)

This is a new edition of the highly influential 'Synthesis Report' (School provision for Gypsy and Traveller children) commissioned by the European Commission and first published in 1986 which led to the adoption of the Resolution on school provision for Gypsy and Traveller Children by the Council and Ministers of Education on 22 May 1989.

September 1998, 310 pages. ISBN 0 900458 88 7, paperback £10

On Gypsies: Texts issued by International Institutions

Compiled by Marielle Danbakli (Interface Collection, Volume 5)

A collection of texts, in a single handy volume, issued by the European Community (the Council and the European Parliament), the Council of Europe (including the Committee of Europe, CLARAE, CAHID and the CDCC) and other international institutions including the Conference on Security and Co-operation in Europe, the United Nations and the UN High Commission for Refugees.

CRDP, 1994. ISBN 2 86565 099 5, 209 pages; paperback £18

University of Hertfordshire Press, Learning & Information Services,
University of Hertfordshire, College Lane, Hatfield, AL10 9AD, UK.

Tel: +44 1707-284654   Fax: +44 1707-284666
E-mail: UHPress@herts.ac.uk

Web catalogue: http://www.herts.ac.uk/UHPress